Ladder of Light

Ladder of Light

The Meaning of the Beatitudes

HAROLD BLAKE WALKER

FLEMING H. REVELL COMPANY

NEW YORK · LONDON · GLASGOW

Copyright, MCMLI, by
FLEMING H. REVELL COMPANY

Special Pulpit Book Club Edition

Printed in the United States of America

51-9442

New York (10): 158 Fifth Avenue
London (E.C.4): 29 Ludgate Hill
Glasgow (E.2): 229 Bothwell Street

TO MY WIFE

Whose continued encouragement
and thoughtful helpfulness
have made this book possible

CONTENTS

INTRODUCTION

No man is great who is not good, for goodness is an indispensable ingredient of greatness. Power degrades both its possessor and those who feel its impact unless it be guided by moral principle. Success that lifts a man to the pinnacle of achievement is a treacherous thing unless it be undergirded by spiritual stability. Distinction in the world of affairs is but a house of cards unless it be infused with moral dignity. Wealth, apart from moral worth, is an invitation to disintegration. Apparent greatness flounders into failure and disillusionment unless it be tempered by goodness.

Ours is a time that demands greatness regnant with goodness. Either we shall live by the ethic of Jesus, finding both peace of mind and social courage in His comradeship, or we shall blunder into a new dark age of misery and despair. Either we shall climb the eight-fold ladder to light implicit in the Beatitudes of Jesus, or we shall meet disaster in both personal and social life. The way to the moral and spiritual greatness our day demands is clear. The summons to climb comes ringing down the ages from the crystal depths of Galilee.

Unhappily, we are thwarted by the fact that the concerted attack in our time upon the ethic of Jesus has overlaid our faith in the Beatitudes and the Sermon on the Mount with a disturbing layer of doubt. We wonder if the Beatitudes are realistic and if they are relevant to the predicament of modern man. In a world of atom bombs and rocket ships, do we dare believe in the power of love and goodness? In our highly competitive culture, dare we risk our lives and our fortunes on the ethic of Jesus?

9

This book attempts to demonstrate that the Beatitudes are both realistic and relevant in contemporary life. Its theme is that the Beatitudes constitute a ladder to light and power to cope with the world as it is, and that they are foundation stones for the "brave new world" of which we dream. The argument begins with the fact of our "egocentric predicament," and our spiritual need if we would manage the "self" creatively. It is based on the conviction that the realism of the Beatitudes is contingent on the "power of the spirit" in the lives of those who answer the Master's call: "Follow me." Without Jesus Christ, the Beatitudes are irrelevant because they are impossible of fulfillment; with Jesus Christ, they are a ladder to moral and spiritual greatness, replete with promise for ourselves and for our world.

As we confront the Beatitudes one by one we are driven again and again to the fact of our spiritual need. The creative mourners, the triumphant meek, the seekers after righteousness, the "pure in heart," the peacemakers, the merciful and the persecuted, all are haunted by their spiritual inadequacy without Christ. In His strength alone are they able to find inner greatness to live out the implications of the Sermon on the Mount. Only as they climb the ladder to light do they enter into the wonder of the larger life in Christ.

These pages have been written, not primarily for the scholar, but for the common reader, for preachers and teachers, for men and women who are eager to live more richly and to find "the power of God unto salvation." They deal with the problems of ordinary living in the light of the Master's creed, which opens the Sermon on the Mount.

I am indebted to Dr. J. Harry Cotton, Professor of Philosophy at Wabash College, for his helpful criticisms and suggestions, to Dr. Joseph Haroutunian, Professor of Theology at McCormick Theological Seminary, and to Miss Georgia Harkness, Professor of Applied Theology at Garrett Biblical Institute, for their kindly suggestions and criticisms. My thanks are due to Miss Betty Flabb and to Miss Mary McClenahan for their careful preparation of the manuscript, and to the congregation of the First Presbyterian Church of Evanston, whose loyalty has inspired creative thinking and constant effort. To my wife I am indebted for continuous encouragement, thoughtful criticism, and infinite patience.

H.B.W.

Evanston, Illinois

Ladder of Light

—◄{ ONE }►—

BLIND APPROACH

THE TENSIONS AND PRESSURES OF MODERN SOCIETY HAVE LED US TO
wonder if the Beatitudes of Jesus are obsolete. Judged by contemporary standards, the Beatitudes bless the wrong people.
The world has no prizes for the "poor in spirit," who feel
the burden of their spiritual need. It is the self-sufficient, the
"go-getters" with boundless self confidence who succeed. They
take the world in their stride and pride themselves on their
ability to "get to the top." They catch the scent of a profit and
pursue it resolutely to its lair. Let weak men talk of need, the
strong are sufficient unto themselves. "Blessed are the meek!"
The world smiles indulgently, as if, somehow, a man should
know better than to expect meekness to "inherit the earth."
Anybody should be able to see that the ruthless make short
shift of the meek. It is the strong who have all the best of
things and the meek who have only what is left. "Blessed are
they that hunger and thirst after righteousness!" The words
read well in print, but in the world of affairs an overdose of
righteousness is quite likely to leave a man hungry and thirsty,
bereft of the blessings of the world.

We are frankly puzzled by the Beatitudes. We have an uneasy suspicion that they have some relevance to our contemporary predicament, and yet they are so out of step with our
ways that they seem unrealistic. As a way out of our di-
lemma, we suggest they represent only an "interim ethic,"
proposed as a pattern for those who expected the near-end of
the world. Or, we imply that our world is so different from

the one that Jesus knew that the beatitudes are out of date. After all, a camel caravan is not exactly a streamlined train and a modern factory has little in common with an ancient potter's shop. The carpenter of Nazareth would be quite overwhelmed by the techniques of modern building. Maybe meekness had some place in quiet Galilee, but modern Chicago or New York are different. The contrast between broadswords and machine guns, between oxcarts and airplanes, is obvious. Modern "hewers of wood" are merely tenders of mechanical saws and contemporary "drawers of water" simply turn a spigot and the public waterworks does the rest. Cæsar's couriers had no Western Union Telegraph, and business men in Antioch had no telephone to Rome. Men lived close to the land in Jesus' day, and the complex problems of distribution of the means of living were mostly unknown.

Nevertheless, for all their outward differences, there is a basic sameness about now and then. Tax-gathering in our time has become a fine art, and yet it is no less painful now than when Jesus said "Render unto Cæsar the things that are Cæsar's." [1] There were tax evaders then—and now. "Let the buyer beware," a word to the wise in our time, had relevance in Jerusalem's market-place. There is no essential difference between a camel, drugged for a sale, and an old automobile "souped-up" to last for thirty days and beyond the expiration of the "guarantee." Watered gasoline and diluted olive oil are at base alike. The hawker selling silks in Athens was an embryonic advertising man. His modern counterpart, who spreads the story of his product by magazine and radio, has the same disposition to exaggerate. While labor unions are new in our time, the injustice that begot them was rife in Jesus' day. No doubt, the men who tended olive groves complained about wages and hours and their employers cursed their complaints. The man who protested to Jesus concerning the division of his father's estate has a thousand counterparts in the courts of our day. Pilate's hatred for the Jews has its

[1] Matthew 22:21.

echo in the anti-Semitism of the present, and the barriers to brotherhood in first-century Palestine are like the barriers we know.

Outward change is obvious, and the increasing complexity of modern civilization has intensified the same problems Jesus faced. The issues of our time are garbed in modern dress, but underneath is man, the same old man whom Jesus knew so well. In the hands of modern man are gadgets that enable him to reach beyond the borders of his sight, and fling the venom of his soul upon the world. His atom bombs, bred from ancient broad swords, have vastly extended the reach of his power. Rocket ships and "superforts" have made the world his parish and expanded his neighborhood. The Apostle Paul walked from Jerusalem to Damascus, intent on destroying Christians; we fly where we will to crush the objects of our hate with high explosives. We have achieved, as Thoreau said, "improved means to unimproved ends." Norman Cousins remarks sadly that modern man has "exalted change in everything except himself." [2]

So, underlying the confusion and tumult of our times, is the same old self that shouted before Pilate's palace, "Crucify him, crucify him." Underneath our agony is the spirit of the silversmiths of Ephesus who clamored against St. Paul when Christian preaching cut their idol-making profits. The cry: "By this business we have our wealth," [3] is as contemporary as the latest news bulletin. Surrounding our social and political corruption is the weakness Paul lamented when he wrote: "Demas hath left me, having loved this present world." [4] Our modern cynicism, disillusionment, and tired idealism are born and bred in the same impatience that made Judas what he was. The struggle for power and preference that breeds conflict has its source in the mood of Jesus' parable of the man

[2] *Modern Man Is Obsolete,* by Norman Cousins, Viking Press, New York, 1945, p. 11.
[3] Acts 19:25.
[4] II Timothy 4:10.

17

who built more and more barns to hold his wealth. Things change; men stay too much as they always have been.

I

Because we have changed everything except ourselves, we are afraid. Basically, we are frightened by the discovery of atomic power because we know we are no better than our ancestors, yet we must handle a thousand times their power. We are afraid because we know we are not good, because our good intentions so easily surrender to our wickedness. Vaguely we comprehend that the dividedness of the world is but a reflection of our inward conflict. Dimly we sense that the issues of history are not decided by parliaments and kings but in the hidden recesses of heads and hearts where men make up their minds "to be or not to be" what God intended. What music we shall have in years to come depends on our choices today between the cheap and tawdry and the great and good. The "New Order" of tomorrow will take its form from what we think and feel today. Our judgments are the frame on which its structure will be hung, our inward sense of values the rock to hold it sure. Thoughts turn into things and worlds in an amazing sort of way, and words, bearing the cargo of the world's ideas, take flesh to dwell among us to build or to destroy.

Norman Cousins is right, then; modern man is obsolete, and not the Beatitudes, for the Beatitudes constitute a creed for new men fit to guide the destiny of our new era. Pride is obsolete, not the humility of "the poor in spirit." Egotism is out of date, not meekness. Sin is as old as Adam, as outmoded as Noah's ark; to "hunger and thirst after righteousness" is the hope of a new era. Hate is an ancient thing, a relic of the days of Cain and Abel, but love is the perpetually contemporary implement of the peacemakers. Cowardice is as old as Pilate washing his hands in a vain attempt to wash out his weakness, while the courage to risk persecution for the sake of righteousness is the trademark of those who alone are competent to build the "brave new world." It is our obsolescence that is the secret of our near oblivion. Our wickedness is behind the wreckage of our world.

The Beatitudes are relevant for our world because they are forever relevant to ourselves. They offer the secret of the soul's competence to manage the self, and we cannot manage our world until we have learned to manage ourselves. We cannot handle our might until we have mastered our truculent souls. If we go on being the same old men, we shall have the same old world of "blood, sweat and tears" on our hands. So the new world will have to begin where the Beatitudes begin, with ourselves and our impotence to manage our own obsolete wickedness. Robert Frost had it right when he summoned us to a "one-man revolution," adding that it is "the only revolution that is coming," [5] indeed, the only revolution that can come. *New social systems mean only a rearrangement of sinners,* so that new hands take over the privilege of doing evil unless inner revolution precedes social revolution. Progress is an illusion unless it has its roots in repentance, in a basic alteration of our motives, purposes, and hungers. Apart from brave new men whose anchors are firm in the heart of God, the "brave new world" will be a mirage.

The Beatitudes of Jesus are the creed for "one-man revolution." They offer at once both a program and a power, a creed and a creative impulse to its fulfillment. They begin with the fact of our spiritual need, our impotence to do as well as we know in the face of our humanness and our involvement in an immoral society. They yield the secret of spiritual strength flowing through the gates of our repentant mourning. They lead us to the facts that undergird the creative and triumphant living of the meek. They sweep away our human dividedness in a divine "hunger and thirst after righteousness," and open the doors to social harmony by way of new men who are

[5] "Build Soil—A Political Pastoral," by Robert Frost, *Collected Poems,* Henry Holt & Co., New York, 1939.

peacemakers. They open the inward eye to the vision of God in whose comradeship there is purity of heart. They fling wide the doors of the soul to moral heroism wherein men stand unfalteringly against the storms of persecution "for righteousness' sake." They are the secret of the soul's integrity and strength.

II

The "one-man revolution" inherent in the Beatitudes involves a revolt against the blatant self-sufficiency of our times and a rebirth of humility that will lead us to seek the wisdom and the will of God. Spiritual pilgrimage cannot even begin until egotism has been reduced to a decent humility. If we hear no voice but that which speaks from the depths of our own will, listen only to the seductive whispering of our own desires, hearken only to the clamoring of our own purposes, we shall be deaf to the still, small voice of God. If we are determined to have our own way, we shall blunder far from God's way. If we think we can manage our own lives and fashion our destiny on our own terms we cannot know the deeper purposes of God. The Beatitudes are nonsense to the self-sufficient, and God is only a respectable encumbrance. If we are wise in our own conceits, we have no use for the wisdom of God.

Our generation, unhappily, has revealed all too little sense of dependence on the grace and the wisdom of God. We are confident in our power, proud of our genius, sure that we are wise enough to manage ourselves and our affairs. Our mood is alien to the spirit of spiritual pilgrimage from a sense of need. Ralph Waldo Emerson described his times as the "age of the first person singular," [6] and the description is not amiss in our day. Emerson was thinking of the Yankee individualism and self-reliance which bred a "devil-may-care" spirit of rugged independence among the builders of the new world. The

[6] Emerson's *Journal* (1827).

pronoun "I" was central in the thinking of pioneer communities, where men lived by their wits and their handiness with a six-shooter. A man took care of "number one" or the coyotes gnawed his bones. In the race to settle new lands a man had to stand on his own feet against all comers. The prizes went to the strong and to the ruthless.

We have refined the age of "the first person singular," but we have the essence of it. We are proudly self-sufficient, quite sure of our capacity to do whatever must be done. "The possible we do at once, the impossible may take a little longer," we say with jaunty cocksureness. Just see what we can do! We can make one hundred thousand airplanes in a single year if the need arise. We can make anything from mouse traps to radar in no time at all. Our "individual initiative" and "private enterprise" are adequate to fill the storehouses of the world with the products of our genius. We have the "know-how" to translate our ideas into things, and we have ideas a-plenty. A man watching automobiles roll from the assembly lines or airplanes pouring from newly-built factories is not inspired to humility. Rather, like little Jack Horner, he is inspired to remark: "What a big boy am I!"

Pride in our power has made us insensitive to our deeper needs. Our genius has given us the illusion of the adequacy of our wits and our wisdom. Our mechanical and industrial finesse have obscured the depths of our ignorance and our moral inadequacy. A visit to the variety store leaves us breathlessly amazed at our own ingenuity. No wonder we assumed that one American was at least as good as ten Frenchmen or a dozen Japanese. Pride leaps from the conviction of genius to the conviction of superiority, without regard for logic. Self-sufficiency all too easily becomes condescension, and even pity. We assume, without asking why, that because we are mighty, we are also good, at least good enough to lead the world to an "American Century." Quite naturally, we conclude that the strong with wits and "know how" have no need of God. Let the weak tend to their prayers; we, the strong, will create new machines and tandem plows to feed and clothe the world.

If we suspect our moral impotence, we hide behind the ramparts of our pride; if we doubt our capacity to "save the world for democracy," or "to make the world safe for peace," we curse the stupidity of other men and resolve to remain aloof from the quarrels of the world. "We have what it takes," to do what we please, and if the world is somewhat skeptical of our self-sufficient genius, the world is blind. If other nations suspect our motives, it is sheer perversity on their part. We know that we are good and we fail to understand why other folk should doubt. Don't we make the "biggest," the "purest," and the "best" of everything? Can anybody make bigger battleships, bigger dynamos, build bigger buildings?

Our genius has obscured our wickedness; our material might has hidden our moral impotence behind a façade of glittering gadgets. Our sense of spiritual need has surrendered to the innumerable evidences of our self-sufficient power. But our very strength is our weakness; our power the symbol of our poverty. Present chaos is evidence of our limited competence; contemporary strife the testament of our spiritual sterility. Strength is weakness until it is infused with the Holy Spirit; wisdom is ignorance until it is regnant with moral reality; righteousness is merely self-righteousness unless it is inspired by One who lived above and beyond the letter of the law. Our genius is our doom unless it be humble and aware of its need for God. Our power has on it the mark of death unless it say: "Not my will but thine be done." Carl Sandburg remarks wisely that "the earth is strewn with the exploded bladders of the puffed up," so the Beatitudes bless the only people who can save us from our strength and redeem us from the stupidity of our self-sufficiency.

III

Our conviction of competence, of self-sufficient genius, has been accompanied by self-righteous pride. It is against such pride that the Beatitudes invite revolt, and wisely, too. The blessed peacemakers necessarily are bereft of Pharisaism and the mood that wraps self-righteous robes around itself and retreats to "splendid isolation." Condescension breeds conflict, and the conviction of moral superiority yields an answering cynicism. The merciful never can be self-righteous, for their mercy stems from knowledge of their own need for the forgiveness of God. "God be merciful unto me, a sinner" is the mood from which all mercy springs and the spirit undergirding social peace. Self-righteous judgment of the sins of others is harsh judgment which comes from playing God and assuming that our judgments are ultimate. There is penetrating insight in the tradition that Satan is a fallen angel who wanted to be God. Innumerable fools throughout history have acted like the devil for precisely the same reason.

"Let no man think of himself more highly than he ought to think" [7] is a word of warning to both men and nations. It is a warning not to identify our own judgments with the judgments of God, for our judgments are quite inevitably prejudiced by our motives and our sins. The Pharisees who brought before Jesus the woman "taken in adultery" stood before the Master with assumptions of self-righteousness, inflated by the sin of the "shady-lady." Jesus altered the pattern of their thinking by making every man look at himself. "Let him that is without sin among you cast the first stone." [8] When the crowd had melted away, self-condemned, He turned to the woman to ask: "Doth no man condemn thee?" Then, with infinite tenderness: "Neither do I condemn thee! Go and sin no more."

That story suggests that self-righteousness cannot endure either honest self-judgment or the deeper judgment of God. It implies, as do the Beatitudes, that in considering our own sins we are to be stern and relentless, but tender and compassionate when we blunder on the sins of others. Indeed, when we are humbly honest we dare not throw stones. We

[7] Romans 12:3.
[8] John 8:7.

know how much there is within ourselves that thwarts the kingdom's coming. What is more, we never know what inward demons our neighbors must overcome, what background makes them as they are. Sally Jones, for example, has a vicious tongue, while my tongue is fairly well bridled. But perchance Sally grew to maturity in a home where her sharp tongue was her defense against prodigal parents, while I grew up in the midst of understanding and love. Bill Williams may be rough, uncouth, and morally indifferent, while I am more or less of a gentleman with a respectable moral concern. Maybe, however, Bill is doing better with his background than I am doing with mine. He had farther to travel than I.

There is a parable of human experience in two streams that flow into the Grand Canyon of the Colorado River. One of the streams is a beautiful, clear, sparkling brook that is a joy to travelers, who pause to watch its plunge into the mighty Colorado. It is called, quite justly, Bright Angel Creek. The other stream is a muddy demon, bearing silt and mud, and nobody stops long to watch it. Appropriately, it is called Dirty Devil Creek. Now, just suppose Bright Angel Creek should find voice and say to its neighbor: "Aren't you ashamed of being dirty and muddy the way you are? You ought to be fresh and clean and beautiful, as I am." The proper answer from Dirty Devil Creek would be: "Is that so? Well, if you had been through what I have been through, you would be dirty too." Amos said something like that to Israel when he felt the gloating of his not-so-pure countrymen. Speaking in the name of God, he said: "You only have I known of all the families of the earth; therefore will I punish you for all your iniquities." [9] Amos was telling his people that considering their heritage, their religious tradition, their upbringing, God had every right to expect them to be much better than their neighbors. To whom much is given, from them much is expected. They had no business judging their neigh-

[9] Amos 3:2.

bors' sins, considering the purifying sands they had known.

It is high time for a "one-man revolution" against self-righteousness, for we are imperiled by our will to judge the world. We deem ourselves the fit, and seek to rule the unfit. There is a tragic similarity between us and our defeated Nazi enemies. They proudly announced their cultural and racial superiority, while we, with equal stupidity, assume our moral superiority, as if we had not sinned against the world we judge. It may well be that, like Cyrus of old, we were instruments of God to destroy the pagan systems of our time, but having served God's purpose, we remain under His judgment. The moment we turn in self-righteous power to be instruments of self-will we are in danger of damnation and disaster.

The spiritual summons of the Beatitudes is for us, pointing to our poverty of spirit and our need for God if we would bear the burden of our power. It calls us to repentant mourning for our sins, and to meekness. It reminds us of our need for the mercy and the forgiveness of God. Humility is our deepest need, and our self-righteous pretentions must yet give way if we would build a nobler world for the generations yet to be. That "pride goeth before a fall" is but an inexorable fact of all human experience. The meek and the humble shall inherit the earth.

IV

The Beatitudes are timely, too, in their invitation to revolt against the mood of self-indulgence that holds us in its grip. We are not here to drift and dream and to please ourselves. The world is not our "bowl of cherries," it is, instead, "a vale of soul-making" wherein we are meant to live lives worthy of immortality. "Straitened is the gate and narrow the way that leadeth unto life" [10] both here and "yonder." The "gate" and the "way" are quite beyond the finding of the self-indulgent who defy the discipline of God. "Blessed are the pure in

[10] Matthew 7:14.

heart" whose single-minded quest for God defies the cheap and tawdry and begets creative power. "Blessed are they that hunger and thirst after righteousness," their random hungers disciplined by the final hunger of the soul. "Blessed are the meek," whose lives are anchored in the purposes of God. The demand for stern self-discipline runs like a silver thread through the Beatitudes, and beside it runs the golden thread of power to fulfill the demands of discipline.

And yet, our mood runs counter to the discipline the Beatitudes imply and to the need our time reveals. The cult of self-expression has played havoc with our inhibitions and led us to believe desires were meant to be satisfied without restraint. We are persuaded that repression begets neurotic twists within the self and that freedom comes by way of letting ourselves go. If we do not like monogamy, and find the bonds of marriage onerous, we think free love will give us peace. We fill our lives with sex and drink as if these things, the fruit of self-indulgence, could make us rich. During the war, we endured taxes and blackouts without complaint, but a ban against night clubs brought a storm of protest. To suggest prohibition is to invite scorn and to be accused of wishing to infringe personal liberty. We demand the right to indulge ourselves.

Our everyday life suggests the extent to which we have yielded to the spirit of self-indulgence. Our whole industrial system caters to our wants, and we demand a wealth of gadgets to make life easy. We mortgage our future to possess the things that make life soft and comfortable. We want education without effort and insight without intellectual industry. We want radio programs that entertain but do not require the slightest effort at attention, and inane motion pictures that enable us to kill time painlessly. We take our exercise vicariously, watching million-dollar baseball teams vie with one another. We give vent to our pugnacity, howling our derision or encouragement on plug-uglies in a ring.

The very word "industry" is rapidly going out of our vocabulary. We are forever wanting less work and more pay without considering how we shall use more time and more money with disciplined creativity. We want to be coddled and pampered and carried along as if the world owed us a living. We can lean on our shovels and loaf on our jobs and collect unearned pay without blinking. The thrift and the industry that drove our fathers toward independence have "gone with the wind" and the tide. We do not even think for ourselves. The radio saves us that trouble. We want security without struggle, comfort without conquest, ease without effort.

Our mood is a dangerous one. The world owes no man a living unless he has shouldered his own responsibility and done his best to bear the burden of himself. There is a striking sentence in the book of Nehemiah at the end of the triumphant story of the men and women who built the walls around the city of Jerusalem—to make the Holy City secure against enemies round about. Nehemiah says proudly: "... we built the wall; and all the wall was joined together: ... for the people had a mind to work." [11] Let no man minimize the significance of that mood. Be men rich or poor, laborers or captains of industry, there is no substitute for "the mind to work" if we would build a nobler future. Indeed, the secret of the sure triumph on earth of the meek is the self-discipline that begets a steady unremitting toil under the light of God. Langston Hughes, the Negro poet, has it right when he says:

> Labor! Out of Labor came the villages
> And the towns that grew to cities.
> Labor! Out of labor came the rowboats
> And the sailboats and the steamboats,
> Came the wagons and the coaches,
> Covered wagons, and stagecoaches.
> Out of labor came the factories,
> Came the foundries, came the railroads.

. . . .

[11] Nehemiah 4:6.

27

Out of labor—white hands and black hands—
Came the dream, the strength, the will,
And the way to build . . .[12]

All this does not suggest that human toil is quite sufficient on its own to build "The City of God." The discipline that leads to creative toil rests on a faith that joyously flings the energies of the self against the inertia of the stubborn earth. It is the faith that there is meaning in our labor, that we are instruments of God and creators in His name. It is a faith that says: "My father worketh hitherto, and I work,"[13] for work I must, to give my life some meaning. If toil is endured only for the sake of trinkets for myself, it is a sterile thing. It is toiling "in Christ's name," and "for his sake" that has a farther reach and gives some worth to hours of labor. Labor for the sake of self-indulgence leaves work without a blessing; and self-indulgent ease robs toil of all its dignity and worth. It is self-discipline, energy chaneled to creative purpose, that yields a benediction.

The Beatitudes are alien to the self-indulgent mood that takes the joy from toil. They are alien to the casualness of so much that we call "work." They would discipline our toil by infusing it with creative purpose. They would fling a ray of light across our barren labor and give it meaning in God. They would beget "the mind to work" for something more significant than bread and gadgets for ourselves. There is a "kingdom not built with the hands" and yet wrought by patient labor in Jesus' spirit. It is "the poor in spirit," aware of their need for guidance as they toil, who build enduring monuments to truth. It is "the mourners," strengthened by the comradeship of Christ, who rise above the cheapness of the self-indulgent mood and create the lasting values of our common life. It is the meek, patiently seeking the facts of

[12] *Freedom's Plow*, by Langston Hughes, Musette Publishers, Inc., Steinway Hall, New York, N. Y.
[13] John 5:17.

28

moral experience and harnessing their lives to creative purpose, who find a blessing in their toil and do at last "inherit
the earth." Those who "hunger and thirst after righteousness"
are constrained to righteous toil. They are disciplined by a
dedication that gathers the energies of the soul and flings
them into life. The "pure in heart" are "singleminded" in
their will to build "the City of God." Not self-indulgence, but
self-discipline marks the mood of the Beatitudes.

The rebellion that devastates our self-indulgence and creates
a kingdom of self-discipline demands the grace of God in
Christ. It is not by sheer will power that we move from wanting what we want to wanting what God wants. It is not by
determination that we infuse our toil with purpose and with
power. The steady "mind to work" and to create the worthy
values of the world is but the flower of our spiritual comradeships. Creative toil that yields a benediction or a blessing
begins with Christ or it does not begin. Self-discipline is not
achieved by tugging at our bootstraps, but rather by catching
some fragment of the trailing garment of Christ and yielding
to his Divine lift. It is he who begets the revolution from
self-indulgence to self-discipline.

V

There is a fourth aspect of the "one-man revolution" suggested by the Beatitudes of Christ which demands the abdica-
tion of our selfishness. The Beatitudes in mood and message
invite submersion of the self and a new focus for desire.
"Not my will, but thine be done" [14] is the theme that runs
through the Sermon on the Mount and is condensed into this
"code of Christ." Greed has no place where God holds sway,
and self-seeking is anathema to the "mind of Christ." Indeed,
the major battle of the Master's life was centered in the selfish
demand of His people for a Messiah who would establish their

[14] Luke 22:42.

priority as temporal masters of the earth. The "chosen people" expected the Messiah to be a soldier, not a servant; they anticipated temporal triumph, not spiritual surrender. Even the disciples were confused by mixed motives, and James and John pleading for the chief seats in the kingdom were victims of the selfish dream of power characteristic of their countrymen.

The current of our times is running strongly against the sacrificial spirit of the Beatitudes. We are driven by the "profit motive," quite unrelieved by any will to spend ourselves without the thought of gain. "What's in it for me?" we ask of those who seek our help in this cause or that. Our service to the community is likely to be somewhat less than self-less. In our honest moments we admit it is "good business." Even the church of Christ does not escape, for there are those who find it convenient to belong for "business reasons." The "call" of the minister to "a larger field of service" may well be somewhat tainted by the size of the salary in the "larger field." We are victims as well as makers of a selfish social system that measures success in terms of profit and power.

Escape is not to be found in social reorganization. Neither socialism nor communism is free from the taint of selfishness. The struggle for power and for profit goes on regardless of the type of economic order. Class pride is a form of selfishness, demanding priority for one group or another. National pride, exhibited in the struggle for favorable economic or military position, is similiar evidence of selfishness. Race pride, which looks with condescension on those who wear a darker skin, is but the testament of our selfish will to have and keep a dominant place within the scheme of things. Like the Pharisees of old, we resent the challenge to the place we hold inherent in the rise of some other race or creed or class. Someone has noted wisely that "there is nothing like a bank account to teach us sound economics," for our soundness is inspired by our fear that radical change will imperil what we possess. A rich man never rocks the economic boat; while the poor man, with nothing to lose and possibly something to gain, is quite willing to see the boat overturned. Selfishness is inherent in the rich and poor alike.

Brotherhood and the sense of community are confronted by barriers erected by the selfishness of men. Even fear of the atomic bomb and the world devastation it betides is not enough to keep the nations from destructive conflicts for place or power. Each nation wants security for itself at the expense of the security of its neighbor, without seeing that security is an idle dream apart from universal brotherhood. Ivor Sikorsky, the Russian airplane designer, put the matter aptly when he was asked: "Is there any defense against atomic bombs carried by rocket planes?" He thought a moment and replied: "None but good will. There is no substitute for good will." But good will is quite impossible so long as selfishness has sway and we are mastered by "the profit motive."

It may be, as secular philosophers contend, that our human dreams of brotherhood are doomed to frustration and to failure in time. Maybe we always shall have wars until all of the combatants are dead or incapacitated. And yet, there is a shred at least of hope that men will find a deeper motive than selfishness and learn to say with Jesus: "My meat is to do the will of him that sent me." [15] The hope is in the "one-man revolution" against selfishness that places God on His rightful throne within the human heart. Unselfishness is not human virtue. It is divine. Mere preaching in favor of it is quite vain. Denunciations of greed are futile to halt the reign of greed. Orations against pride will never end its sway. We have to start with Christ and be transformed by His presence in ourselves before unselfishness can claim our lives. We have to begin with Him or preaching is in vain. Inward revolution, the transformation of motive and desire, begins with Christ and then moves on to brotherhood and community.

[15] John 4:34.

Self-sufficiency, self-righteousness, self-indulgence and selfishness, these four are the demons of our time. They are part and
parcel of our human nature, of our "original sin," and they
are more than we can manage on our own. The Beatitudes
constitute the only creed there is for dealing with these things
within ourselves. They offer a creative technique for personal
revolution and renewal, and, beyond technique, they offer
power. Quite inevitably, they begin with our poverty of spirit
and our all too-evident incompetence to manage ourselves and
our world.

TWO

BEYOND THE FLATLANDS

It is apparent even to the casual observer that the devil-in-chief of our time is the unsubdued self. The self as we know it has its fulcrum in my concern for me. The word "ideology," so common in our times, is indicative of a self-centered philosophy that seeks to organize the world around the selfish desires of men and nations. Ideologies are exclusive, finding the significance of life in the triumph of one group or another, appealing to the pride and the selfishness of those whose lives revolve around my concern for me. Our ideologies, focused in the pronoun "I," inevitably issue in conflict and confusion. The "I," being ultimate, finds no bridge to span the chasm to other "I's," no common allegiance significant enough to overcome dividedness. The "I," being quite final, finds its morals in expediency and its ethic in utility. Absolutes are dead; long live relativity.

The alternative to ideology is theology, wherein life is organized, not around my concern for me, but around my concern for the will of God. The word "theology" has heights and depths never sounded by the word "ideology." It is indicative of a God-centered philosophy that enlists the common allegiance of a multitude of "I's," luring them to a righteousness far beyond "the little aims that end with self." It suggests a way of thinking that shatters the pride and the self-righteousness of the selfish and the self-indulgent. In the light of a worthy theology the will of God is final. Good and evil cease to be relative to ideological ends. Right and wrong are not to

33

be determined by their usefulness or by their capacity to con-
tribute to the selfish ends of the individual or the state. Good
and evil, right and wrong are absolutes whose stern imperatives rightfully command the allegiance of men and nations.
Under the sway of theology, relativity is dead; long live the
absolute.

I

The first Beatitude has its roots in theology, in the priority
of God. It lifts us above the flatlands of self concern. It offers
a blessing, not to the proud, whose lives revolve around the
orbit of themselves, but to the "poor in spirit," whose motives
find their fulcrum in the will of God. It promises the kingdom
not to the self-sufficient, who press toward goals of their own
creation; but to the humble, who march to the music of God.
The "poor in spirit" are the self-emptied, whose prayers echo
from Gethsemane: "Not my will, but thine be done."[1] They
are the dynamic creators of the everlasting good, who lose
themselves in devout dedications, forget themselves in sublime causes, abandon themselves as "fools for Christ's sake."[2]
They are the free who escape the perils of self-affirmation in
self-surrender. They live, not by ideology, but by theology, by
"every word that proceedeth out of the mouth of God."[3]

When I was a boy going to Camp Chief Ouray, near
Granby, Colorado, the motto of the camp was: "The other
fellow first." It was an apt motto, and we lived up to it fairly
well, except at meal time. Then someone with a theological
turn of mind suggested that the motto be changed to, "I'm
third." The idea behind the change was that God should
come first in our thinking, others next, and ourselves last. The
change was made in the motto, and, at least in slogan, we
joined the ranks of "the poor in spirit." In our thinking we
had become conscious of the fact that we had no business

[1] Luke 22:42.
[2] I Corinthians 4:10.
[3] Matthew 4:4.

being first, even though we had difficulty pushing ourselves out of God's way.

The poor in spirit are those who have succeeded in getting themselves out of God's way. They take no pride in their own prerogatives and demand no special concessions as their right. They do not push or shove to the head of the line when somebody has to wait. They are not social climbers, intent on making a name. They are more interested in principle than in power, more concerned about righteousness than riches. They want truth more than triumph and honesty more than honors. They rejoice in the triumphs of others and offer their congratulations without envy. The praise they bestow is unspoiled by critical reservations. They are abundantly serious in their conviction that "I'm third." Since they do not stand in their own way, they do not get in God's way.

The "poor in spirit" do not wear their feelings on their sleeves. They are not easily hurt because they are not forever haunted by my concern for me. They "see life steadily and see it whole" because their thinking is not colored by excessive self-interest. They dare to be objective. In the midst of conflict they are peacemakers because they are able to divorce themselves from the issues and see the right as God sees it. They dare to risk themselves for righteousness' sake because they do not matter too much to themselves. They are the Niemoellers who prefer concentration camp to compromise, the Jane Addamses who would rather be persecuted for righteousness' sake than be popular in moral surrender. They know and live by the conviction that they are third.

The "poor in spirit" live by a perspective that is not self-fouled. The meaning of events, they know, is not to be found in what happens to them. History is something more than a personal matter, so that even in the midst of disaster their faith is unspoiled. They see far deeper than the girl, evacuated from London during the "blitz," when bombs threatened the destruction of the city. Howard Spring describes her reaction

35

with penetrating insight into our human predicament. She tried to study in the new school, but:

> Canute bored her; you could keep Henry VIII so far as Vi'let was concerned; and she would have made a present of Magna Carta at any time to anyone who wanted it. Now, for the first time in her life, without knowing that she knew it, Vi'let knew what history meant: it meant what happened to Vi'let Lovell.[4]

If history means merely what happens to me, then history has no room for faith or hope. Creativity is sterilized by despair and self-preservation is the only law of life. Egocentric history is meaningless history, with neither compass nor magnetic pole. God-centered history, however, is meaningful history in which the individual is the instrument of a Will beyond his own and a Purpose more significant than his own little aims and wants. The stability of "the poor in spirit" hinges on their spiritual perspective, on their faith that God is Lord of history, and on their knowledge that what really matters is what happens to the will of God. Hence their poise in the midst of world earthquake and storm, and their faith in the triumph of righteousness both in and beyond history.

II

Despite their goodness and virtue, "the poor in spirit" are characterized by the fact that they know they are not good. Though they are abundantly righteous by the standards of the world, they are not self-righteous. They are spiritual princes without pride and moral conquerors without condescension. Though they be humble, they are not proud of their humility. They know themselves too well to be deceived by the outward cloak of goodness which the world sees. Inwardly they are aware of a strange depravity which only God can

[4] *Social Insight Through Short Stories,* Edited by Josephine Strode, Harper & Bros., New York, 1946, p. 194. Excerpt from "An Evacuated Child," by Howard Spring.

master. Despite their will to say: "I'm third," they know they
are perpetually a battle ground between "the flesh" and "the
spirit." Like Charlie McCarthy, they are "torn between vice
and versa." They know that salvation lies not in the will, but
in the power of God, that self is not easily subdued, and that,
as George Meredith said of mountain climbing, "every step
you take is a debate between what you are and what you
might become."[5] They, like the rest of us, are "bound in the
bundle of life," with "one foot in heaven" and the other securely anchored to the earth. The very fact of the struggle
is enough to damn their self-righteousness and inhibit their
moral pride. The fact that so often they want to be first when
they know they ought to be third is enough to convict them
of participation in "original sin," and to remind them that
they are not good.

It should be noted, of course, that even the good man never
altogether escapes the seductive lure of evil deeply embedded
in himself. He never is wholly free from the tempter. St. Paul
did not attain the sublime estate of comfortable security in the
good. He complained to the end of his days that the "principalities and powers" against which he wrestled were mighty
indeed, thwarting the good he wished to do. The legendary
picture of Luther hurling an ink bottle at the devil bears the
stamp of psychological realism, testifying to the tension of the
tempted good. To be sure, the character of a man's moral
dilemmas changes as he approaches moral maturity and joins
the ranks of the "poor in spirit"; but his temptations merely
become more subtle and therefore more dangerous. The pull
of the less-good, if not the positive evil, remains to plague
the saint and to remind him that he is not good. Indeed, the
saint frequently finds his tension more acute because his moral
sensitiveness is more fully developed than the sinner's. The
finer the spirit, the sharper the conscience; the higher the ideal,
the more poignant the failure to achieve it. Be we good as

[5] *Pilgrims' Way*, by Lord Tweedsmuir, Houghton-Mifflin Co., New
York, 1940, p. 132.

saints or pure as angels, the demoniac in human nature is present to affirm the limited character of our goodness.

The genius of "the poor in spirit" inheres in the fact that they know they are not good, while most of us are easily persuaded we are good enough. The "poor in spirit" are conscious of their inward wickedness, while the average man is likely to be proud of his rectitude. Consequently, the "poor in spirit" are deeply conscious of their need for the power of God to make them better, while ordinary men are reluctant to acknowledge their spiritual need. Indeed, one of the most disturbing attitudes of our time is that which is expressed in the comment: "My religion is the Golden Rule. I try to be honest and fair and to do right by my family and my community. I think I am as good a Christian as anyone I know." Those who speak thus are unaware of the fact that their moral pride is decisive evidence that their ego has pushed God from His rightful throne within.

The most devastating criticism Jesus ever leveled at men was hurled upon the Pharisees. He called them "whited sepulchers." Why? They were not bad, they were good; they were not evildoers, they were fundamentally righteous. Their difficulty lay in the fact that while they were righteous, they were self-righteous. Jesus, someone remarked, could love anyone but a Pharisee. In their goodness the Pharisees were loveless, in their correctness they were condescending, in their pride they were unaware of their spiritual poverty. Pity the moral pride of the Pharisee who prayed in the market-place: "I thank thee, Father, that I am not as other men are, extortioners, unjust, adulterers, or even as this Publican," [6] and then went on to remind God that He fasted, not once, but twice each week and that he tithed not only his income but all he possessed. Unhappily, the history of religion displays on every page the sad spectacle of men swollen in the conceit of their own righteousness and proud of their humility. They are the

*Luke 18:11.

38

very antithesis of "the poor in spirit" who for all their good-ness know they are not good.

III

It is because "the poor in spirit" start with God and not with themselves that they come to an awareness of their inadequate goodness. Most of us start with ourselves and the world and so find it possible to escape condemnation. Screwtape, the devil, as he is pictured by C. S. Lewis always is seductive enough to remind us that someone else is much worse than we are. We escape from the judgment of God by way of the more tolerant judgments of man. Our pride is nourished by the sins of our contemporaries. Our moral deportment may deserve only a mediocre "B," but there are a host of men who merit only a "C." To be sure, we may be momentarily humbled by the presence of a moral Phi Beta Kappa who makes us seem a little on the seamy side, but we hurry away to the company of "birds of a feather" so that we may bask in the comfort of moral comparison.

The "poor in spirit," however, find no comfort in the sins of their contemporaries. They stand in the judgment of God and know they stand condemned. They do not harm their enemies; but they know they do not love as their Master loved. They commit no adulteries but they know their minds are not altogether pure. They do not steal, but they are aware that they covet. They do not bear false witness, but they know the reality of their jealously. In humility they confess:

> We have erred and strayed from Thy ways like lost sheep. We have followed too much the devices and desires of our own hearts. We have offended against Thy holy laws. We have left undone those things which we ought to have done and we have done those things which we ought not to have done.[7]

[7] *Book of Common Prayer*, Protestant Episcopal Church.

They know their confession is the sober truth, and they know it to be the truth as a consequence of their theology which confronts them with the judgment of God.

There is no humility adequate to save us from the devil-in-chief of our time except that which centers in the judgment of God. If we judge ourselves, we excuse ourselves, and take refuge in the luxury of alibis. If we are judged by the world, we are judged by the mediocre morals of the mob. If we are judged by our friends, we are misjudged by their prejudice in our favor. There is no road to genuine humility save that which leads to the unrelenting judgment of God. There is no trail to the blessedness of "the poor in spirit" except that which takes us before the throne of the living God. Even Jesus traveled that road to humility. He rebuked the young man who came running to ask, "Good Master, what shall I do to inherit eternal life?" "Why callest thou me good?" the Master said in answer. "There is none good but one, that is, God." [8] "The judgments of God are sure and righteous altogether." [9] In the light of such judgment we see ourselves as we really are and we are humbled.

Reinhold Niebuhr has overstated the truth in his observation that "the only moments in which the self-righteousness is broken are moments of genuine prayer." [10] It is true, however, that in moments of honest prayer our self-deceptions are unmasked and our pretenses are punctured. Apart from God, we are able to deceive ourselves and excuse the sins which so easily beset us. Without God to bother our bovine complacency, we can belittle the evils of society in which we are involved. But in the presence of the Ultimate Goodness, even our denunciation of the evils of the depraved are saved from the stupidity of self-righteousness. We know that both the righteous and the wicked stand under a judgment more ulti-

[8] Mark 10:17-18.
[9] Psalm 19:9.
[10] *Discerning the Signs of the Times,* by Reinhold Niebuhr, Chas. Scribner's Sons, New York, 1946, p. 18.

mate than that of the moment. When we stand under the judgment of God we know the old hymn had it right,

> Just as I am, without one plea
> But that Thy blood was shed for me,
> And that Thou bidd'st me come to Thee
> O Lamb of God, I come, I come.[11]

Our hypocrisies fail us and our vindictive judgments shame us in God's presence. Our self-righteousness is broken by the judgment of God, and we are humbled and "poor in spirit."

It is not only the judgment of God but also the grace of God that humbles "the poor in spirit." The extravagant benevolence of God in the face of our sins and stupidities is an unending source of humility. The assurance of forgiveness when we do not deserve to be forgiven; the promise of mercy when we have no right to mercy; the confidence of love that will not let us go, even when we would flee from His presence are amazing gifts we do not, cannot earn. They leave us humbled, yielding to His will and love. "God commandeth his love toward us, that while we were yet sinners Christ died for us" [12] was Paul's way of saying what "the poor in spirit" feel with grateful wonder.

The Prodigal Son, coming home after "wasting his substance in riotous living," found the wonder of a father's love unspoiled. He could but say in the agony of a humble confession: "Father, I have sinned and am no more worthy to be thy son." [13] The lad coming home from moral failure and finding a mother's love still strong and sure is constrained to whisper in anguish: "Mom, I'm just no good." So "the poor in spirit," knowing the reality of their sin before God, yet seeing in Jesus Christ the unfailing, unfaltering character of the Father's love and compassion, are driven to humility. They know the meaning of the well-loved hymn:

[11] Charlotte Elliott.
[12] Romans 5:8.
[13] Luke 15:18.

O Love that wilt not let me go,
I rest my weary soul in Thee.[14]

Who can be proud in the presence of the judgment and the grace of God? What does a man possess that has not been given him? Paul wants to know. And if it was given, why should we boast as if it were gained, not given?[15] We did not earn our talents. We did not achieve our I.Q. We did not make sunsets or evening stars or all the wondrous beauties that are joys forever. Our capacities came to us by grace. George Eliot used to say nothing she ever wrote was hers. It was really handed to her. She merely reached out and took it. Our insights are more revelation than reason, more given than achieved. We really do not know what is our own, and what we have we know we did not altogether earn. The "poor in spirit" sense their debt to the grace of God and have the wit to live more like guests than proprietors in the world.

Ernest Colwell remarks significantly that "the God who is the source of Jesus' humility is a God of grace."[16] Jesus was Himself "poor in spirit" in response to the benevolence of God. "The Son can do nothing of himself,"[17] He acknowledged. He did not speak for Himself; He spoke for God. His wisdom was not His own; it was God's. His power was not His own; it was God's. He never even pretended to be on His own. He was what He was because God was what He was, and God was in Him. "He that believeth on me," He remarked, "believeth not on me but on him that sent me."[18] His goodness was God's goodness and His truth was God's truth. If He dared to say, "I am the way,"[19] it was because He was going God's way, not His own. He was humbly "poor in spirit" in response to the grace of the Father.

[14] George Matheson.
[15] I Corinthians 6:20.
[16] *An Approach to the Teachings of Jesus,* Ernest Cadman Colwell, Abingdon-Cokesbury, New York, 1946, p. 81.
[17] John 5:19.
[18] John 12:44.
[19] John 14:6.

IV

When life is centered in the will of God and confronted by the judgment and grace of God it is driven to its need for God. Dr. Edgar Goodspeed, in his translation of the New Testament, suggests that the "poor in spirit" are those who "feel their spiritual need." As Schliermacher suggested, they are aware that they are absolutely dependent on God. It may well be that Luke's more blunt recording of the first Beatitude finds its ultimate meaning in the quality of spiritual need which poverty infers. "Blessed are the poor," [20] says Luke, as if to say, "Blessed be nothing." But Luke's word is no blanket affirmation of the blessedness of poverty. It is rather a suggestion that poverty may awaken an awareness of spiritual need, whereas prosperity frequently obscures the needs it cannot satisfy. The rich man gets stuck going through the needle's eye to the kingdom, not simply because he is rich, but because his riches all too easily stuff him with spurious values and leave him with a bloated ego. Wearing the clothing of riches and power, it is all too easy to forget that "clothes do not make the man" and to rest the security of the self on the outward favors of society. James M. Barrie understood the truth when he wrote *The Admirable Crichton,* a play in which a small company of Britishers were shipwrecked and stranded on a South Sea Island. There, with the favors of aristocratic society stripped away, it was the butler who turned out to be the man and the nobleman who turned out to be something less than noble. The lord and his spoiled daughters had been getting by on their position and were "all outside, no inside." The security of their social position had obscured the insecurity of their spiritual foundation.

Jesus marveled at the rich and well-born who achieved spiritual maturity. "With men," he said, "this is impossible, but with God all things are possible," [21] as if only God could save

[20] Luke 6:20.
[21] Matthew 19:26.

the rich from the spiritual corruption of their riches. He understood all too well that those who are holding their own or getting ahead in the competitive struggle for the means of living are not so likely to be oppressed by their own inadequacy as those who are overwhelmed and defeated in the struggle. The successful have more to overcome on the road to spiritual maturity than the unsuccessful. Spiritual need is less obvious in a penthouse than in a tenement house, and a sizeable bank account frequently obscures spiritual bankruptcy. "Where your treasure is, there will your heart be also." [22] is a realistic reading of experience, suggesting that material wealth claims the heart and closes it to the treasures of the spirit. There is a close relationship between material comfort and spiritual corrosion!

Basically, however, wealth and poverty are neutral. There are the humble rich and the proud poor. There are those who defy the pride of riches with an abiding sense of their spiritual need, and there are those who translate their poverty into resentment against a society that refuses to take them at their inflated self-estimate. There are those, too, who cloak their poverty with a spurious humility like that of Diogenes, who visited Plato, and finding the philosopher pleasantly housed, stamped on the luxurious rugs and exclaimed: "Thus do I trample underfoot the pride of Plato." Shortly thereafter, Plato returned the visit and found Diogenes living in ostentatious poverty. He observed with ironic realism that he could see the pride of Diogenes "peeping through the holes in the carpet." The rich and the poor alike may be victims of the pride which obscures spiritual need. The "poor in spirit," in rags or riches, are those who are aware of their sin, their weakness, their inward dividedness and their desperate need for God.

[22] Matthew 6:21.

44

V

It is "the poor in spirit," emptied of ego and keenly aware of their spiritual need, who inherit "the kingdom of heaven." That kingdom is not so much the reward as the possession of "the poor in spirit." No matter what Jesus meant by the "kingdom of heaven," whether it be a future abode, a present reality, or an inward state, it has to begin inside ourselves. We do not blunder into heavenly blessedness after a life of self-made hell. Father Smith had it right in his meditation concerning the ways of his people:

> Of course they wouldn't all go to hell any more than they would all go to heaven. There was purgatory, wherein the weak and the worldly were made clean, because even the best of men couldn't hope to go clod-hopping straight into God's presence after spending a lifetime talking about umbrellas and colds in the head.[23]

We do not stumble into paradise after a life indifferent to the claims of God. We do not create Utopia outside until we have ordered our lives inside. The "kingdom of heaven" is a vain dream of wishful thinkers until we possess it inwardly, until by self-emptying we have opened our souls to the God of judgment and grace.

There is no royal road to "the kingdom of heaven" by way of material values, however intriguing. Quality has no substitute! Human experience is like that of a child busy with his crayons, coloring an outdoor scene in which several cows are grazing in a meadow. Unable to find the brown crayon, he colors the cows a bright purple. In the end, however, the picture, flaunting its purple cows, is exotic. Cows ought to be brown or black or even white, but never purple. The purple is an offense against reality, a feeble attempt to substitute an irrelevant color for an honest brown or black. It does not satisfy. It offends. So it is that our material substitutes for

[23] *The World, The Flesh, and Father Smith,* by Bruce Marshall, Houghton-Mifflin Co., Boston, 1945, p. 3.

45

spiritual values leave us cold—offended and unsatisfied. They are as meaningless and out of character as purple cows. They lead us not to "the kingdom of heaven," but to the vast empire of cynicism. There is, as Jesus understood, a "spiritual need" which is quite beyond the reach of our human devices and substitutes. The truth is strikingly suggested in Herman Melville's words:

> The world clean fails me;
> Still I yearn.[24]

That we are aware of the stupidity of our self-indulgent quest for material substitutes for values that lead to the kingdom is suggested by the popularity of a machine often seen at county fairs and designed to enable a man to kick himself. We actually are willing to pay for the privilege of giving ourselves "a swift kick well placed." We honestly enjoy the chance to kick ourselves because we know quite well that we deserve to be thrashed in one way or another. We are aware that we should have known the world would fail us, leaving us to yearn for the abiding treasures of the human heart. Like Byron and Shelley, the "Romantic Rebels" of another generation, we taste the flavor of the world only to find it bitter and weighted with sorrow and boredom. As Byron noted,

> The thorns which I have reap'd are of the tree
> I planted; they have torn me, and I bleed.
> I should have known what fruit would spring
> from such a seed.[25]

Byron and his comrades should have known that the fruit of the spirit would not spring from the sins of the world. Their tragedy lay in their failure to perceive the spiritual character of their yearning. Success, position, prestige—all these were theirs. But they turned away from the searching question,

[24] *Clarel,* by Herman Melville, quoted from *The Story of American Literature,* by Ludwig Lewishon, Harper, New York, 1932, p. 193.
[25] *Childe Harold's Pilgrimage,* by Lord Byron, Hurst & Co., New York, Canto IV, Stanza 10.

"What lack I yet?" [26] They would not listen to Augustine saying across the ages that they always would be restless, yearning, troubled, until they found their rest in God. They would not believe that the kingdom of heaven belonged only to "the poor in spirit."

The kingdom of heaven and its blessedness elude all but "the poor in spirit." The proud may well win the kingdom of the world and wear the scepters of temporal power. The selfish and the self-indulging may taste the fruits of the material world, but their triumphs are tasteless for their devil-in-chief is their doom. In the end, the world clean fails them and they yearn for something quite beyond their reach. They do not understand, as do "the poor in spirit," that both sovereignty and serenity come only through surrender. They do not comprehend that there is life in theology, death in ideology.

Over and over again, Jesus insisted that only those who are lifted above themselves are sovereign over themselves; only those who surrender to the will of God are serene within themselves. In the garden where He wrestled with His soul and God, He uttered the deepest word of His message; "Not my will, but thine be done." [27] To His disciples He said: "Whosoever of you that renounceth not all he hath, he cannot be my disciple." [28] And again, "What shall it profit a man if he gain the whole world and lose his own soul?" [29] With strange paradox, He insisted, "He that findeth his life shall lose it, but he that loseth his life for my sake, the same shall find it." [30] So, triumphant living comes by way of surrendered living, for "everyone that exalteth himself shall be humbled, but he that humbleth himself shall be exalted." [31]

We may push through the days stubbornly demanding our own way if we please, but we had better remember that Satan got to be Satan by trying to be God; he was cast out of the

[26] Matthew 19:20.
[27] Luke 22:42.
[28] Luke 14:33.
[29] Mark 8:36.
[30] Matthew 10:39.
[31] Luke 14:11.

kingdom of heaven for trying to have his own way. Most of us blunder into conflict and confusion and hell on earth for the same reason. As Whittier put it,

> To turn aside from Thee is hell,
> To walk with Thee is heaven.[32]

Life was meant to be lived on God's terms, not ours. It was meant to be lived by theology, not ideology. The truth was brought home to me a little while ago when a small boy handed me two metal rings puzzlingly linked together and said, "I'll bet you can't get them apart." He was right, of course. He watched me in silence some little time. Then he shook his head, took the rings and slipped them apart with the greatest of ease. He handed them back, and I began anew the twisting and turning. He said, guiding my hands, "You do it this way, not that way," and when I did it "this way" the links fell apart in my hands. After half a dozen tries, I learned to take the links apart and put them together unerringly.

My experience with those rings, puzzlingly linked together, is a parable of all life. While I was trying to separate them on my own terms, I blundered into frustration, failure, and a sense of irritating futility; but when I surrendered to the guidance of a small boy and tried the right way, I was sovereign over the rings. When I willed the boy's will, I discovered the rightness of his way. It was inherent in the very nature of the rings. They were made to come apart and go together but one way. That one way always worked, and there could be no success apart from surrender to the will of him who made the rings work that way.

Jesus is like that small boy, knowing a simple secret. He is forever saying, as we blunder through our days meeting frustration and failure: "Do it this way, not that." But He goes on to add that "the way" He proposes is not really His way, but God's. It yields sovereignty and serenity because the uni-

[32] John Greenleaf Whittier.

verse is made the way it is. We can blunder on if we please, trying to have our own way, to live with ourselves at the center of things, or we can surrender to His way, to His love, to His judgment, and find the only peace there is, the only kingdom worth possessing.

Gerald Heard, echoing the *Theologica Germanica,* remarks pertinently that "nothing burns in hell but the ego."[33] He is right. Nothing keeps us from God's way but the ego; nothing drives us to the stupidity of our self-seeking but the ego; nothing drives us to inward and outward conflict but the ego. Omar Khayyam put the truth discerningly in his lines:

> I sent my soul into the invisible,
> Some letter of the after-life to spell.
> And by and by my soul returned to me,
> And answered, "I myself am Heaven and Hell."[34]

Quite so. We always are in hell save when we are out of ourselves. Our lives are one blundering stupidity after another except when they are yielded to a Will beyond our will and a Spirit wiser than our own. We are hurt by the sharp edges of the universe and bruised on hard tablets of stone save when we are "poor in spirit." But in surrender we are sovereign over ourselves; in surrender we are serene and strong. Humbled by the judgment and the grace of God, we are exalted by His strength and guided by His wisdom to a kingdom not built with hands.

Nevertheless, we blunder on burdened by our wickedness, making the world not a garden but a grave. We struggle on as did St. Augustine, refusing to love God and yield to His will until our lament must be akin to Augustine's:

> Too late I loved Thee, O Thou Beauty of ancient days,
> yet ever new! Too late I loved Thee! And behold, thou

[33] *The Code of Christ,* by Gerald Heard, Harper & Bros., New York, 1941, p. 25.
[34] *Rubaiyat of Omar Khayyam,* Illustrated Editions Co., New York, p. 186.

wert within, and I abroad, and there I searched for Thee; deformed I, plunging amid those fair forms, which thou hast made. Thou wert with me, but I was not with Thee. Things held me far from Thee, which unless they were in Thee, were not at all . . . when I shall with my whole self cleave to Thee, I shall nowhere have sorrow, or labour; and my life shall wholly live, as wholly full of Thee. But now since whom Thou fillest, Thou liftest up, because I am not full of Thee I am a burden to myself.[35]

Until we become "poor in spirit," the kingdom is far from us and we are a burden to ourselves.

But if we dare to stand before the judgment and the grace of God in the humility of the "poor in spirit" we shall be filled with "the power of God unto salvation." C. S. Lewis puts the truth simply in *The Screwtape Letters* when Screwtape, complaining against God, the Enemy, remarks:

Of course, I know that the Enemy also wants to detach men from themselves. . . . He really likes the little vermin, and sets an absurd value on the distinctness in every one of them. When He talks of their losing their selves, He only means abandoning the clamour of self-will; once they have done that, He really gives them back all their personality, and boasts (I am afraid, sincerely) that when they are wholly His they will be more themselves than ever. Hence, while He is delighted to see them sacrificing even their innocent wills to His, He hates to see them drifting away from their own nature for any other reason.[36]

So, "Blessed are the poor in spirit, for theirs is the kingdom of heaven." Even the "devil" knows it is true.

Well knowing the satanic power of the human ego, Jesus moved on to speak of mourning, of the moment of devastation which by its shock may help tear away the last shreds of pride and lead us by sure steps to the comfort and the peace of God.

[35] *Confessions of Augustine*, E. B. Pusey, ed.
[36] *The Srewtape Letters*, by C. S. Lewis, Macmillan Co., 1944, p. 68.

THREE

THROUGH VALLEY AND SHADOW

THE SECOND BEATITUDE, "BLESSED ARE THEY THAT MOURN: FOR they shall be comforted," [1] marks the second step on the road toward self-conquest. It speaks to our need when we go down into "the valley of the shadow," where we become aware of what de Unamuno calls "the tragic sense of life." Suffering and sorrow, retribution and regret close in upon us and we feel the weary weight of our own incompetence to manage our days. Our self-assurance blunders into the rough edges of the universe and we come away knowing our need for the assurance of God. Our self-indulgence sends us floundering into the misery of the morning after and we feel the burden of our guilt. Our self-righteousness muddles into mistaken vindictiveness whose issue is lamentation and regret. Our selfishness pushes us blindly into conflict whose evil flings itself upon the just and the unjust alike. We know in the midst of our mourning that we are not big enough to stand up to life altogether on our own. The dark waters of despair close over us and we know we are done without God.

On the face of things it seems absurd to congratulate a man who is floundering. Nevertheless, Jesus greets the mourners with a word of congratulation, as if to suggest that men ought to be blessed by the tempering of the tragic. In the face of our rebellion against the blows that strike us down, the Master invites our discovery of the creative ministry of our mourning. He disturbs the course of our bitterness with the

[1] Matthew 5:4.

51

suggestion that beyond the blows that beat us down there is a blessing to be found; on the other side of our tears is a triumph to be won. There is nothing sentimental in His thinking, and He never tells us naively that the blows we suffer are not really as hard as they seem. Not for a moment does He suggest that pain and suffering are only errors of mortal mind. Indeed, He insists, "In the world ye shall have tribulation." [2] Jesus suffered cruelly, but quite obviously there was creative power in His pain, for as the writer of Hebrews affirmed, "Though he were a Son, yet learned he . . . by the things which he suffered." [3]

There was a delightful bit of wisdom in the spontaneous comment of a small boy who walked into a lovely chapel one afternoon when the sun was streaming in through the stained glass windows. "Oh, Mother," he said, "aren't the windows pretty?" Then, after a moment of silence, he added, "Even the ones I don't like are pretty." That remark goes deeper than it seems on the face of it, for most of the things we do not like have their worthy sides. We do not like sickness or sorrow, disappointment or pain, the retribution of our sins or the failure of our fortune, and yet they all contain possibilities of value for us. Even the things we do not like possess elements of spiritual beauty if we see them with the light of God shining through. So Jesus knew when He spoke hopefully to the mourners.

I

There are times, of course, when our mourning is quite profitless, and there is no assurance that sorrow will be redemptive. Sorrow may be altogether devastating. Mourning often turns to bitterness and leaves us with a sterile cynicism. There are those who incur the judgment of Dante, as having "wilfully lived in sadness," for there is a narrow margin between mourning creatively and muddling from mourning

[2] John 16:33.
[3] Hebrews 5:8.

to self-pity. Mourning gets nowhere unless it gets us to God. The world sees no possiblity of beauty in the hurts and calamities that fall upon us; without God, evil is unmitigated by any hope of transforming grace.

Walt Whitman deeply felt the alternatives when, during the tragedy of the Civil War, he wrote of the

> Year that trembled and reel'd beneath me!
> Your summer wind was warm enough, yet the air I
>   breathed froze me,
> A thick gloom fell through the sunshine and darkened me,
> Must I change my triumphant song? said I to myself,
> Must I indeed learn to chant the cold dirges of the baffled?
> And sullen hymns of defeat? [4]

"Triumphant song" or "cold dirges" and "sullen hymns of defeat," one or the other will emerge from the mourning of the hurt, the baffled and the sorrowing. But surely, the singers of "cold dirges" and "sullen hymns" never are tempered by the tragedies of life. No triumph ever came to men of shattered faith whose frustrations made them cry, "I am undone." No city of the living God ever reared its spires from the ashes of our burned-out hopes. Only the brave, held together by the fabric of their faith, have won the togas of triumph and heard eternal voices saying to their souls, "Well done."

Mourning is both a peril and a promise: a peril if it flounders feebly through the days bereft of God; a promise if it leads the hurt to see the shadows of their individual hurts and disappointments against a background of eternal strength. Suffering and sorrow can be creative if they lead us to the strength beyond our strength. The word "comfort" in the second Beatitude suggests the meaning of mourning that is blessed, for the word comes from two Latin roots, *cum* (with) and *fortis* (strong). Jesus really said to the multitudes:

[4] *Drum Taps and Sequel to Drum Taps,* by Walt Whitman, quoted from *Walt Whitman,* by Edgar Lee Masters, Charles Scribner's Sons, New York, 1937, p. 114.

"Blessed are they that mourn: for they shall be provided with strength." There is, however, a vital "if" implicit in the promise. The blessing of strength is assured only if the mourners face up to their spiritual need and seek God in their mourning. The hurt discover then that God's comfort means not cushions, but courage; not pity, but power. The Greek of the New Testament suggests a kindred ministry of mourning. The New Testament speaks of God, the Holy Spirit, as the Paraclete, and in the King James Version, Paraclete has been translated "comforter," which weakens its import. "Counselor," as the New Revised Version has it, is better. The Beatitude may be read: "Blessed are they that mourn: for they shall have the Holy Spirit alongside of them." The comforter is the Holy Spirit, who comes along to make strong.

The tragedies that beget mourning lead us to bitterness because we miss the reality of the Holy Spirit coming to us with strength. Like Baudelaire, we know the devil in fact but we know God only in theory! We have a curious feeling that God ought to keep us from our hurts and comfort us with safety and security, forgetting that God is intent on making something of us. No doubt there are times when He yearns to save us from the follies that lead to mourning, and from the hurts that tear us apart. John Wesley even spoke of "the prayer of God," the anguished prayer of One who loves and yearns for us to do His will and so avoid unnecessary hurts.

We who have watched children learning to walk know all too well what a temptation it is to pick them up, hug them and kiss them when they fall. Parents would give a great deal to be able to teach their children to walk without the bruises and the bumps. And yet, the secret of helping a child to learn the art of walking and the key to shaping his attitude toward life is in letting him pick himself up from the floor. To be sure, we will stand by, encouraging, perhaps offering a finger for leverage. But to coddle is to weaken, to cushion every fall with fluttering concern is to destroy the dawning

54

strength of body and spirit. It was Rousseau, the French thinker, who, concerning one dear to his heart, said:

> I shall not take pains to prevent Emile hurting himself; far from it. I should be vexed if he never hurt himself, if he grew up unacquainted with pain. To bear pain is his first and most useful lesson. Instead of keeping him mewed up in a stuffy room, take him out into a meadow every day; let him run about, let him struggle and fall again and again, the oftener the better; he will learn all the sooner to pick himself up.[5]

God is like a wise parent, standing by, hurt by our hurts, wishing, like Jesus, to gather us "as a hen gathers its brood," yet knowing He must let us take bruises and hurts and sorrows for our own soul's sake. He is in the shadows offering inward dignity and strength if only we will reach out as a child reaches for the finger that will help him to his feet again. "Behold I stand at the door and knock," [6] is a realistic reading of our spiritual experience, but we bolt the door as we might against the old-time salesman of brushes and shoe laces. We do not sense that it is love we are locking out, the stabilizing, strengthening, enduring love of God. "Blessed are they that mourn: for they shall be comforted" if they open the door to God.

There is a human analogy to the way we close the door on God, an analogy which will help us to see our spiritual selves. All of us have noticed that there are times when our children shut the door in our faces. Something goes wrong, they run headlong into experiences they do not like and retreat into themselves. Love, no matter how compassionate, cannot penetrate the wall they build around themselves. They will not let us inside, but rather hold us at arm's length until we feel helplessly impotent. We know they are hurt about something,

[5] *Emile,* by Jean Jacques Rousseau, from *The Living Thoughts of Rousseau,* presented by Romain Rolland, Longmans, Green & Co., New York, 1939, p. 87.
[6] Revelation 3:20.

that some unidentified wound is festering inside. Behold, we stand at the door and knock, but we cannot get in to help because they, with curious perversity, will not open the door. We adults are exactly like our children, which explains a large portion of our human conflicts and disasters. Husbands shut doors against their wives and wives slam doors in their husbands' faces. Our friends—God knows we would like to help them face the hurts of their days—but inexplicably they lock us outside and we turn away sadly, knowing we have failed. They would not let us lend them of our strength in their need. We were ready with love, compassion, and friendship; we wanted to give so much of ourselves. It was they who shut the door. In some such strange fashion we close the door on the love of God. Wounded by our sorrow, bruised by our tragedies, hurt by our moral failures, we brood in sulking resentment, refusing to reach out in humble trust for the hand of God. There seems to be nothing pretty about our plight and we retreat somberly into the shell of our self-contained mourning. It is not that God does not come to lend us of His loving strength; it is rather that we close the door on the comfort of His Holy Spirit.

Death is no tragedy in itself; moral failure is by no means final, and material loss or physical calamity are not unmitigated disaster if in the moment of mourning we open the door to the living spirit of God. "Blessed are they that mourn," not because they are overwhelmed by sorrow, not because life has tumbled in one way or another, but only if in their spiritual need they open the door to the strength and the fortitude and the peace of God. "Blessed are they that mourn: for they shall be comforted."

II

Quite commonly we mourn our sins the morning after we have faltered in the face of our moral tensions, and we resolve "never again." Our mourning, however, is quite futile until it becomes "godly sorrow for our sins." That is quite different from hang-over regret, wherein we mourn not our sin but our headaches. Sin has no redemptive side until it becomes, as Paul said, "a means of grace," until in godly sorrow we open the door to the strength and dignity of God. The struggle of St. Augustine is instructive at this point because it suggests the pattern of our own behavior. When Augustine finally "came to himself," he understood for the first time that sin is sin and polite rationalizations were quite unable to make it anything else. He was haunted by the face of his newly-discovered Lord and Master and quite honestly he wished to follow "the way." Nevertheless, as his *Confessions* suggest all too plainly, there was a disturbing memory of the pleasures of yesterday which gave his sins a rosy cast. When he cried in his familiar prayer; "O Lord, give me chastity, but not now," he sought a nullification by postponement. He mourned, and yet he did not mourn his sins. He was weary of "morning after" regret, and yet he could not forget the satisfaction of the night before. He was not sure whether he preferred the feeling of guilt along with his sins, or the inward peace of commitment to his Christ. He had to make up his mind and turn in godly sorrow from his sins, sins of the flesh and also sins of pride and ambition, before he could find the grace that was sufficient to keep him strong and pure. He had to mourn honestly before he could find the blessedness of the Comforter's strength. So it is with all of us.

The significance of the "day of adversity" lies in the fact that it often leads us to "consider" ourselves with realism and to sense the misery of our dividedness and our inadequacy to meet it with positive power. Like as not, suffering is sin that is finding us out and adversity the revenge of unrepented evil. To be sure, not all suffering stems from sin, but our deepest misery does. When we are brought low, to "sackcloth and ashes," and our worldly hopes have played us false, our sense of need is clearer than it is in penthouse prosperity. Our sins seem less alluring in rags than in riches and we are more keenly aware of the retribution of wrong. The feeling of aloneness is poignant then; the sense of alienation from the living God descends like an impenetrable fog. It was the sense of aloneness and alienation that finally overwhelmed Augustine and drove him to his choice between his sins and Christ. It was the terrible lonesomeness of life in "a far country" that in the end drove the Prodigal Son home to his father's house.

It is this wanting to share the fellowship of Christ and to belong again to the commonwealth of God that is the essence of repentance, the dynamic for "letting go" of our sins. In the dark hours of life we mourn not only our sins, but also the devastating lack of sustaining spiritual fellowship. We can endure suffering; we cannot endure loneliness; we can face adversity, we cannot endure alienation too. Father Chizzom spoke the truth when he remarked in *The Keys of the Kingdom,* "The defeated still have everything if they still have God." [7] So the repentant in their distress find everything if in their mourning they find the Comforter who stands beside them in their need. Their sin becomes, then, a means of grace and power, their dividedness the inspiration of a new unity in Christ. They know they are forgiven and cleansed.

What is more, the comradeship of the Comforter begets moral power to do and dare righteously. The word of Immanuel Kant, "I ought: therefore I can," presupposes reliance on the strength of the Comforter. It assumes that "godly sorrow for our sins" has opened the door to the Holy Spirit, who comes to our side to aid us with His strength. God gives us the right to defy our moral imperatives, but He lends His hand of strength that we may rise stronger than before. The comfort of His Spirit is, indeed, blessed to those who mourn their sins.

[7] *The Keys of the Kingdom,* A. J. Cronin, Little, Brown and Co., New York, 1941, p. 290.

III

There is, too, another type of mourning that is both peril and promise. It is that mourning which comes when the fates strike us down with illness or ill-fortune. The fates themselves are neutral; we may be their victims or their victors. Beethoven, become deaf, resolves to "seize fate by the throat," and his biographer says of him, "We are eternal debtors to his deafness," for he used his mourning to make abiding music. Helen Keller, struck blind, deaf and dumb, wrote a symphony of beauty with her life. On the other hand, Lord Byron, gifted with great genius, but afflicted with a club foot, left spiritual ruin and bitterness in his wake. As Trelawny observes, Byron's lameness made him "skeptical, cynical and savage." [8] Mourning was the anvil, but each furnished the hammer that fashioned the soul.

In the end, it is not the blows of fate that break us apart. Goethe noted wisely that "we are our own devils; we drive ourselves out of our Edens," [9] and it is so. We turn our hurts into the devil of self-pity; we transform our outward defeats into inward demons of despair; we take our tragedies and translate them into "cold dirges" and "sullen hymns," while the devil laughs. Indeed, we are "our own devils" because we determine the meaning of the blows which befall us; we interpret the harsh clutch of circumstance and say what it shall mean to our souls. Speaking of a Southern gentleman who broke under the adversity of the Civil War, one of Margaret Mitchell's characters comments, "He could be licked from the inside. I mean to say that what the whole world could not do, his own heart could." Then the simple philosopher goes on, "There ain't anything from the outside can lick any of

[8] *Trelawny*, by Margaret Armstrong, The Macmillan Co., New York, 1940, p. 210.
[9] *Goethe, The History of a Man*, by Emil Ludwig, G. P. Putnam's Sons, 1928, p. 18.

us." [10] We write our own tickets to our destiny, and that destiny depends on whether we mourn creatively or destructively.

Pitirim Sorokin's book, *Man and Society in Calamity,* is a stirring epic, picturing as it does how men and women through the centuries have dealt with war, pestilence, tragedy, and famine. Always there are those who go to pieces. Embittered, brutalized, broken, they pour their poison into the stream of humanity. But in every calamitous generation there is a steady "remnant." Their hurts are the motive for their gentleness, their wounds are the dynamic of their self-sacrifice, their sorrow is the power behind their social passion. They take the ruins and the wreckage of their dreams and build a bridge to span the tide of woe and reach to better days. Gloriously they deal with themselves, knowing they "cannot be licked from the outside." By the grace of God, they turn their mourning into a ministry.

The secret of the noble fruit of mourning is, indeed, discovery of the strength of God. There is, to be sure, a certain weather wisdom in the fatalism of Taoism as it is reflected in Lichtse's parable of "The Old Man at the Fort," as recorded by Lin Yutang. But the reading will suggest that Jesus goes far deeper into the need of the human spirit.

> An Old Man was living with his son at an abandoned fort on top of a hill, and one day he lost a horse. The neighbors came to express their sympathy for this misfortune, and the Old Man asked, "How do you know this is bad luck?" A few days afterward, his horse returned with a number of wild horses, and his neighbors came again to congratulate him on his stroke of good fortune, and the Old Man replied, "How do you know this is good luck?" With so many horses around, his son began to take to riding, and one day he broke his leg. Again the neighbors came around to express their sympathy,

[10] *Gone With The Wind,* by Margaret Mitchell, The Macmillan Co., New York, 1936, p. 711.

and the Old Man replied, "How do you know this is bad luck?" The next year, there was a war, and because the Old Man's son was crippled, he did not have to go to the front.[11]

There is a vast difference between the stoic fatalism of the Old Man at the Fort and the transforming dynamic of the Christian faith. *One accepts outward events with resignation and the gratitude of despair; the other seizes fate by the throat and makes music of it;* one merely "takes it," the other makes something of it; *one mourns without hope, the other mourns with creative power.* Most of us find it quite impossible just to absorb blows and to take the good and the evil that come upon us with resignation. We wear down in no time just standing in a corner warding off blows and lamenting the fates that make things so. We have to advance, to march onward or we are done, as Jesus understood when He replied to those who warned Him of the fury of Herod, "Nevertheless, I must go my way today and tomorrow and the day following."[12] Pushed into a corner, Jesus took the offensive. He wept over Jerusalem, but He pushed on against the sins of Jerusalem which were destroying the souls of men. Such always is the strategy of those who weep with wisdom. They press on doing hard things, noble things in spite of the ache of their hearts.

It is here, in pushing on in spite of things, that Jesus goes far beyond mere philosophy. There is, He insists, a power that goes beside us in our hurt, a "Comforter" who makes us strong to do and to dare if we feel our spiritual need and lift up our eyes with the expectation of vision and courage to see us through. There is a suggestion of what the Holy Spirit does in an experience of my high-school days, when the glee clubs presented Gilbert and Sullivan's *Mikado* at the Denver City Auditorium. I was by no means an outstanding Poo Bah.

[11] *The Importance of Living,* by Lin Yutang, John Day Company, Inc., New York, 1937, p. 160.
[12] Luke 13:33.

There was one solo that gave me no end of trouble, and I found it quite impossible to sing the part on key. I could sing it with the piano, but when the orchestra joined the fray, I became thoroughly lost. Then, the night of the dress rehearsal, Manuel Galea, the pianist, came to me and said, "Don't you worry about that solo. Listen for the piano and I'll play the melody instead of the usual accompaniment for your solo." That was like an oasis in the middle of the desert for me. Then came the night of the performance and the moment for my solo. I stood before the footlights trembling as the orchestra began the strains of my solo. Then I heard Manuel thumping the piano, doing what he said he would. I sang my solo that night and I stayed on key, because the piano sang with me.

It is so that the Comforter stands by us, keeping us on key through storm and struggle. In the moment that we mourn the fates that plunge us into situations beyond our depth, demanding competence greater than our own, the Holy Spirit comes with strength if we open the door for His coming and in humility confess our spiritual need. "Blessed," indeed, "are they that mourn: for they shall be made strong." In that coming of the Comforter to strengthen us there is beauty even in tragedy and hurt.

IV

Beyond mourning our sins and lamenting our disappointments, limitations and hurts, there is the mourning that comes to all of us as we face the death of our loved ones. Death is one of life's great and mysterious inevitables. When we say the word "life" we imply its opposite "death." When we speak of "joy" we infer its contrary "sorrow." Life has meaning only in contrast with death and joy has significance only in relation to sadness. The Scriptures are forever explaining life or death, joy or sorrow in terms of their opposites, as if one were meaningless without the other. The Psalmist finds God turning "mourning into dancing," [13] and Isaiah sees God substituting "the oil of joy for mourning" and "the garment of praise for the spirit of heaviness." [14] George Matheson caught the truth when he wrote:

> O joy that seekest me through pain
> I cannot close my heart to thee.[15]

Christianity, with the realism of God, sets the Cross of Calvary and the open tomb of Easter morning side by side.

There is an inevitableness about sorrow, and nothing can alter the fact that rain falls upon the just and the unjust with a blatant lack of concern for who gets wet. Sorrow comes, and comes alike to all, for

> Time, like an ever rolling stream,
> Bears all its sons away.[16]

Mothers and fathers, brothers and sisters, beloved friends, husbands and wives slip from our grasp into that land beyond the sunset of our knowledge, where faith alone can reach. We cannot live without sorrow, without days of sadness when we walk down into "the valley of the shadow of death" with someone we have loved.

We had better lay the foundations of our thinking and our faith, then, upon the inexorable fact of sorrow. "He was a man of sorrows and acquainted with grief" [17] is a realistic statement of truth for all of us. Let it be noted, however, that it is not the whole truth, as multitudes are wont to assume. Jesus was seeing life "steadily and seeing it whole" when He said, "Ye shall be sorrowful, but your sorrow shall be turned into joy." [18] Tragedy inheres in the fact that so many of us stop with the fact of mourning and refuse to press on to its

[13] Psalm 30:11.
[14] Isaiah 61:3.
[15] *O Love That Wilt Not let Me Go.*
[16] Isaac Watts, 1719, *O God, Our Help in Ages Past.*
[17] Isaiah 53:3.
[18] John 16:20.

other side, where there is joy in new-found strength and poise beyond the shadows. We are poor, indeed, if we fail to find the ministry of God hidden in the sadness we dislike.

The ministry of God in our sorrow is a ministry of meaning, for the love of God is the source of our assurance that death is not doom but a daring adventure into the beyond. It begets an inward trust that death is but the threshold of life, the dawn of deathlessness, wherein the unfinished is finished and the fragmentary is made whole. It inspires an overflowing faith that there is a future with God wherein we shall see, not as "through a glass darkly," but "face to face." Our night is lighted, as by a candle at first, and then as by a shaft of light from Eternity. We stand for a while in the dark of our despair until our eyes begin to see. Little by little, we cease our petulant desire for any comfort save the assurance that God is and cares.

The kingdom forever, beyond the shadows of time and tide, is but the logical outcome of the love and goodness of God. "For God so loved the world, that he gave his only begotten Son, that whosoever believeth in him should not perish, but have everlasting life," [19] suggests the eternity we shall have beyond the world to make things right as they were never fully right before. Life and death find new meaning in the fact that the future does not stop with our passing from the world's small stage. It reaches far beyond the horizons of our seeing, for life is not just a bubble blown by a playful creator for his own amusement. Life does not explode into nothingness at death, leaving no trace of its glory. "I am the resurrection and the life," said Jesus. "He that believeth on me, though he were dead, yet shall he live." [20] Then, with a smile, He asks: "Believest thou this?" So, in the midst of our mourning, we are constrained to believe that beyond this life there is more life, and beyond the kingdom of this world is a kingdom forever with the Father.

[19] John 3:16.
[20] John 11:25-26.

We talk glibly now and then of "pie in the sky," as if immortality meant residence in some kingdom of perpetual self-indulgence. We sing with a smirk:

> I'll be where loud anthems are always a-ringing,
> But as I've no voice, I'm clear of the singing.
> Don't mourn for me now, don't mourn for me never,
> I'm going to do nothing, forever and ever.

I want none of that, but in the providence of God I want a kingdom beyond wherein I can finish the saga of my soul. I am so blind, and there is so much I want to see. My ignorance haunts me, and there is so much I want to know. My goodness is so fragmentary, and I want to be so much better than I ever can be in this feeble frame of mine. If the chance to go on growing "in grace and in the knowledge of our Lord and Saviour Jesus Christ" [21] is eternal life, it is what I want. If the chance to finish the unfinished symphony of my soul, to be rid of the discords and disharmonies in it, is what comes after this life is done, then I want it.

When today has been lived and its mistakes cannot be mended, when today is done and its hurt cannot be healed, when today has been ended and its waste cannot be altered, we need the kingdom forever to make things right. There is so little time, too little time, unless we have an eternity to grow, unless we have forever to make the symphony sound like a symphony. What is there left to redeem the wreckage today unless we have a future with God, and a chance to be ourselves in the kingdom beyond?

If in the moment of our mourning we are impelled not to resentment but to search for spiritual reality, we shall find a ministry of meaning in God. We shall find poise in the spiritual significance of death, unfailing assurance in the goodness and the love of God. We shall know that our loved ones do not die; they go on to complete their incompleteness.

[21] II Peter 3:18.

"Blessed are they that mourn," for they shall find meaning in life and in death.

The ministry of God in our sorrow is not only a ministry of meaning, it is also a ministry of perspective. "O Zion, that bringest good tidings, get thee up into the high mountain." [22] The devastation of sorrow lies in the fact that it is my sorrow, all mine. The small moment crowds out memory of the joys of yesterday and the possibilities of tomorrow. We live too easily in the grim shadows of the valley, forgetting to climb up to "the high mountain." We become enmeshed in our own misery, forgetting the whole of which our misery is but a part. William Allen White used to say that he enjoyed the radio comments of Hendrick Van Loon on the day's events "because he made them seem like a part of a whole, not an isolated moment in time." [23] Our difficulty with sorrow is that it becomes so easily "an isolated moment in time." There is a halting of time in sorrow when we see nothing but the awful present, divorced from the past and the future. There is a breaking of the anchor chains that hold us to the living flow of personal and social history. Our sorrow is the isolated event, the island surrounded, the moment of great aloneness. Perspective perishes in "the isolated moment in time." We weep for ourselves in our aloneness. Tears flow because we feel the heavy burden of loss that is terribly our own.

God does not begrudge us our tears when sorrow comes. He is not unmindful of our anguish and of our right to emotional release in tears. We are not made of steel, insensitive to the blows that befall us. We weep because we must and in the hour of our bereavement we are tortured. But we rob death of its redemptive power for us if we cling to our tears. We miss the ministry of mourning if we cling resolutely to our sorrow and will not climb the high mountain where we are able to see life clearly again. But if we climb to "the secret

[22] Isaiah 40:9.
[23] *In Praise of E. B. White, Realist,* by Clifton Fadiman, *New York Times Book Review,* June 10, 1945.

place of the most high," [24] the "isolated moment in time" falls into the perspective of history. It takes its rightful place in the stream of time and meaning as a source of creative power and insight. Then we discover as did Charles Lummis: "I am bigger than anything that can happen to me. All these things—sorrow, misfortune, suffering—are outside my door and I have the key." [25] We are bigger than anything that can happen to us because we are a part of something bigger than ourselves; we are segments of a whole in which we play a worthy part.

One of the most stirring passages in Browning's "Paracelsus" describes how, with tired feet, he toiled onward, discouraged, nearly broken, and then caught a vision of the Celestial City in the distance. The isolated moments of his distress lost their power to destroy him, and the vision that linked him to the whole course of his life reinforced him to go on. Says he:

> I remember well
> One journey, how I feared the track was missed,
> So long the city I desired to reach
> Lay hid; when suddenly its spires afar
> Flashed through the circling clouds; you may conceive
> My transport. Soon the vapors closed again,
> But I had seen the city, and one such glance
> No darkness could obscure.

Then comes the climax of his insight:

> Nor shall the present,
> A few dull hours, a passing shame or two,
> Destroy the vivid memories of the past.
> I will fight the battle out; a little spent
> Perhaps, but still an able combatant.

When, under the ministry of God, the small moment falls into the perspective of the vision of a goal and a promise of a

[24] Psalm 91:1.
[25] *Epigram,* by Charles Fletcher Lummis.

destiny we find poise and courage to fight the battle out with dignity. The small moment is not all there is.

There was a sublime faith about the way Columbus sailed his little ships from Spain to the new world in 1492. Misfortune, contrary winds, mutinous crews were outside his door and he held the key. His men were sure the wind never would blow them back to Spain, so when on September twenty-second the wind changed, Columbus wrote in his diary: "This contrary wind was of much use to me, because my people were all worked up, thinking that no winds blew in these waters for returning to Spain." Columbus knew little more than his men about the winds on the unexplored sea, but, as Samuel E. Morrison suggests, "his serenity came from an inward assurance and confidence in God, not from superior knowledge." If the seas ran high and battered his little ships, he would manage; if calm came in the wake of a storm he would write, "Thanks be to God." [26] He was better, at least on that voyage, than anything that could happen to him, because in the moment of trial he climbed to the high mountain of God to see that contrary winds and favorable winds alike were helpful to his cause. Fair winds and foul were but part of a whole, creative in its total impact.

Such is the ministry of God in our sorrow. Standing atop the high mountain, we begin to see that contrary winds minister to our courage and our faith, that by way of our sorrow we grow richer in spirit and more mellow. What is more, we begin to comprehend that the meaning of our sadness is to be found in the creative use we make of it. Indeed, so far as our own lives are concerned, the only meaning inherent in the death of a loved one is to be found in what we do with death. If we blunder into bitterness from the perspective of the dark valley, we rob both the life and the death of our dead of their creative significance. If we wander aimlessly through the days in weeping and lament, we steal the spiritual power from the

[26] *Admiral of the Ocean Sea,* by Samuel E. Morrison, Little, Brown & Co., Boston, 1942, p. 206-7.

once warm hands of our loved ones. But if, like Middleton Murry, when his wife, Katherine Mansfield, died, we seek "the secret place of the most high," we come to understand that "the All Great" is the "All Loving too." In that discovery we march on steadfastly to honor our dead and give meaning to their passing. In God, the dead can enrich and ennoble the living. From the perspective of the high mountain, sorrow can be a creative experience for those who must go on living.

The ministry of God in our sorrow is, then, a ministry of meaning and of perspective, but it is also a ministry of transforming power. God's comfort is a creative thing that overflows into a new dynamic for sympathy and human helpfulness. It takes the bereaved to comfort the bereaved, the disappointed to encourage the disappointed, the hurt to help the hurt. When we walk into a dark room it takes a while for our eyes to adjust to the darkness. Go into a motion picture theater from the sunlight outside, and you need somebody who has been there a while to show you a seat, otherwise you may sit on somebody's lap. Those who have known sorrow are like those who have been in the dark long enough to see, and to show us the way through it. That is part of the glory of the Christian faith—the sorrow of God, who "gave his only begotten Son." [27] It was sorrow magnificent in its creative power, breathing dignity and courage and strength into the lives of the disciples, creating a church, stirring the soul of mankind, opening the doors to a new era of history. Calvary's cross is the profoundest symbol there is of the sorrow of God overflowing into understanding, compassion, and strength for human kind. The cross is an everlasting symbol of the transforming power of sorrow.

Your sorrow and mine may be like unto God's, flinging a benediction on the lives of those whose hurts have left them broken and crushed. It has been the men and women of sorrow "acquainted with grief" who have been the greatest

[27] John 3:16.

69

servants of mankind. One of the most stirring illustrations of the truth is to be found in an address by John Bright which describes the experience that drove him to a career of understanding service:

> "I was in Leamington," he said, "and Mr. Cobden called on me. I was then in the depths of grief—I may almost say of despair, for the light and sunshine of my house had been extinguished. All that was left on earth of my young wife, except the memory of a sainted life and a too brief happiness, was lying still and cold in the chamber above us. Mr. Cobden called on me as his friend, and addressed me, as you may suppose, with words of condolence. After a time he looked up and said: 'There are thousands and thousands of homes in England at this moment where wives and mothers and children are dying of hunger. Now, when the first paroxysm of your grief is passed, I would advise you to come with me, and we will never rest until the Corn Laws are repealed.' " [28]

The experience of John Bright has been repeated unnumbered times. There was Hosea, finding in his own sorrow the key to the salvation of his people. There was Beethoven making music, Milton writing sublime poetry, Florence Nightingale healing the hurt, as if somehow there had to be sorrow on the heart before there could be music on the lips. Clearly, God's comfort in our sorrow means transforming power.

V

Life is, indeed, burdened with regret, misfortune, and sorrow, but the mourners know that as they carry on "today, tomorrow, and the day following," they can count on God for meaning, perspective, and power. "I intend to conquer at

[28] *The Book of the Twelve Prophets,* Vol. I, by George Adam Smith, Doubleday, Doran & Co., Inc., 1929, p. 253.

least my own little foot of territory afresh each day," [29] said
Goethe, with a fine awareness that "God helps those who help
themselves." Nevertheless, he had no wish to bear the weight
of years that "trembled and reel'd," with God on a protracted
vacation. He had to know, as we do, too, that "the everlasting
arms" are real enough to hold us in our need, that the tears
of God mingle with our tears.

Too often we go to pieces, mourning with destructive bitterness, because we think that when we have finished conquering
our own little foot of territory each day we have finished.
What saved the prophets and St. Paul, the saints and heroes
of yesterday was their faith that when they had finished, God
was just ready to begin. When they came to the end of their
rope, they knew God's hand would hold them fast; when their
crosses had them groggy, God would lend His strength to see
them over the hill. They did not have to take the worst alone.
They could count God in.

When we go to pieces and blunder into bitterness our behavior is a commentary on our faith, or lack of it. We think
we can manage our sins and our hurts and our sorrows by
ourselves if we just try hard enough, but that is not the case.
Too often we try too hard and go on the rocks for all our
trying. Too proud to surrender to our spiritual need and to
mourn with the door open on our side of God, we flounder.
Like a frightened boy trying to learn to swim, we struggle
until we sink from sheer exhaustion. All the while we ought
to know how easy it is to float, sustained by a glorious buoy-
ancy whose generous strength knows no limitations. His
Everlasting Arms are no figment of the imagination, they are
real as the stars are real. To be sure, we do not find their
security until we dare to lean on their strength in humble confession of our need; but, then, did ever a beginner believe the
water to be his friend? What fearful splasher in the shallow
end of the pool ever believed the water would not let him

[29] *Goethe, The History of a Man,* by Emil Ludwig, G. P. Putnam's
Sons, New York, 1928, p. 90.

sink? He strikes off into the deep water only when he dares to trust.

"Blessed are they that mourn" and trust, for they shall be made strong. Paul knew it was true when he wrote with great gratitude and from his own experience: "Unto him who is able to do exceeding abundantly, above all that we ask or think . . ." [30] Paul found something magnificent on the other side of his mourning. It was enough to make him, as he said, "more than conqueror." [31] It is enough for us, too, if we seek God with all our hearts.

[30] Ephesians 3:20.
[31] Romans 8:37.

FOUR

THE OTHER SIDE OF CÆSAR

THERE IS NOT MUCH ARGUMENT ABOUT THE FIRST TWO BEATI-
tudes. They stick fairly close to the realm of the spirit, dealing
with spiritual need and spiritual comfort. The third Beatitude
has a down-to-the-earth flavor and runs into a storm of contrary opinion. "Blessed are the meek: for they shall inherit the
earth." [1] Just get rid of that business about inheriting the
earth; let the meek inherit the kingdom of heaven, anything
but the earth, and the realists will not object. But, as it stands,
it is too much for the "tough-minded." Their tone is incredu-
lous when they ask: "You mean the meek will inherit the
earth? Don't be stupid. Don't you know that

> Force rules the world still,
> Has ruled it, shall rule it;
> Meekness is weakness,
> Strength is triumphant,
> Over the whole earth
> Still is it Thor's-Day! [2]

I

Of course, there is something to be said for that point of
view if we make the mistake of thinking of meekness as weak-

---

[1] Matthew 5:5.
[2] *The Saga of King Olaf*, by Henry Wadsworth Longfellow, from
Tales of a Wayside Inn, The Complete Poetical Works, Houghton
Mifflin Co., Boston, 1893, p. 69.

ness. As a matter of fact, however, there is nothing weak about the meek. Only the strong can be meek; only the tough can be tender. Just look at Jesus. Can you imagine the man who "set his face steadfastly to go to Jerusalem" and dared the fury of His enemies without flinching, promising the earth to the weak? Jesus was meek, but never weak. There was a quality of tempered steel in His soul that conquered without coercion, that triumphed without violence. He wore no crown except a crown of thorns, and waved no scepter of temporal power, and yet kings and empires have perished before the inexorable march of His power. William Lecky is right when, in speaking of military power, He remarks:

> . . . the strongest
> Often do not last the longest.[3]

In his contests with Jesus, Cæsar has come off second best. Such was the conclusion of T. G. Masaryk, the great founder of the Czech Republic, who concluded two of his books with the words, "Jesus, and not Cæsar . . . this . . . is the meaning of our history and democracy." [4] No, meekness is not weakness—never.

The truth is evident as we travel back along the corridors of time to see the ruin of the kingdoms of blood and iron. One after another, the Assyrians, the Babylonians, the Greeks, the Romans, the Manchus, the Germans took the sword and perished by the sword. The Pharaohs and the potentates, the Cæsars and the conquerors have passed away amidst violence and bloodshed. "The stars fought against Sisera," [5] even as they have fought all through history against the tyrants who sought by violence to enslave the human spirit. The meaning of history is to be found in the triumph, not of the mighty but of the meek. We cannot escape the testimony of history:

[3] *Of an Old Song,* by William E. H. Lecky, from *The World's Great Religious Poetry,* Macmillan Co., New York, 1944, p. 10.
[4] *The New Europe* and *The Making of a State,* by Thomas Garrigue Masaryk.
[5] Judges 5:20.

God is on the side of the meek and against the terrible striv-
ings of the mighty.

What is more, meekness, as Jesus understood it, is not softness, either. It is not a willingness to be pushed hither and
yon by the swirling tides of the world. "Peace at any price"
was not the motto of Jesus. "I am come," He said, "to send not
peace but the sword." [6] There was no peace for Him. Indeed,
He had no place to lay His head. He was a focal point of storm
and strife, a rock on which breakers shattered themselves. He
conducted no armed campaigns; He was, rather, the anvil
upon which evil wore out its hammers. His sword was raised
against no man; but the swords of many were broken against
the sword of His unconquerable spirit. There was nothing of
the softness of appeasement in His soul; there was rather the
strength of eternal judgment. Now and always, men judge
not Jesus but themselves by their answer to the question,
"What think ye of Christ?" [7] So, the meekness of Jesus was
not softness, it was unconquerable strength.

II

What, then, is meekness? James Moffatt suggests one aspect of it when he translates the passage to read, "Blessed are
the humble-minded: for they shall inherit the earth." Such a
reading helps us get behind the scenes to the source of the
power that inheres in meekness. Humble-mindedness implies
a passion for the facts which undergird life, an open-minded
receptivity to the realities of human experience. "Ye shall
know the truth," said Jesus, "and the truth shall make you
free." [8] It was His way of telling us to build our lives on
foundations of truth and fact. It was an invitation to pilgrimage in pursuit of abiding and unfailing realities.

There is a suggestion of the spirit of the humble-minded in

[6] Matthew 10:34.
[7] Matthew 22:42.
[8] John 8:32.

the story told by Hal Hibbert, designer of the P-38, the fighter plane that made history in the early days of the Second World War. In the Fall of 1937 a new four-engined plane was being tested for aileron flutter. Somehow, the control mechanism failed and the motor "ran away." Structural failure resulted, and the plane began to disintegrate. Six of the seven-man crew parachuted to safety. The seventh was the flight engineer, who stayed at his post to describe in writing what happened. Men on the ground had to know what the plane would do, and where it needed strengthening before it could go into production. He wrote: "Control to motor failed; motor speed increased from 350 to 750 rpm, aileron fluttering. Airplane speed increasing now to 310 miles per hour. Aileron has fluttered off. Wing is now gone. Spinning." Then, having recorded these facts, he saw it was too late to jump. He wrote, "Sorry," and crashed. His comrades had the following legend inscribed on his tombstone: "He gave his life for the facts." [9] Men had to know the truth about that plane before they could risk it in combat with other planes, so "he gave his life for the facts."

Life is like that plane. It cannot stand the strain of combat, struggle, and strain, unless it is anchored to and guided by a knowledge of the facts about it. It will not stand up under stress if it is built on prejudice, on unexamined opinion or untried theory. The meek and the humble-minded are those who seek with abiding passion to know the truth about life and to build the structure of their lives on foundations of moral and spiritual fact. They are the teachable, who go beyond appearances to the realities underneath. They listen with patience to the record of what happens to life under strain as it comes from one who endured every test on the way to Calvary. They are responsive to the voice of the spirit speaking through the law and the prophets. They crave the truth about life.

[9] Hal Hibbert, Emporia College Commencement Address, 1943.

Meekness is the natural destination of one who has traveled the road of spiritual pilgrimage through poverty of spirit and mourning. When we have emptied ourselves of pride, our untested opinions lose their authority and when we have faced our incompetence to meet life triumphantly we are ready to accept the guidance of Reality. The humble mind is the mind aware of its spiritual need, conscious of the necessity for anchors in God's truth. The prejudices and the outworn traditions of the world lose their coercive power and become what they really are. Attitudes and dispositions are to be tested by something deeper than our human feelings; they are to be judged in the light of Galilee. Meekness is the testament of our escape from the grim clutches of ourselves, the evidence of our trust in the final reality of truth in Christ. Let it be noted, too, that meekness is realism of the soundest sort, cutting away the superficial bellowings of the self; for the self, shorn of its egotism, aware of its spiritual need, rests its security on facts that will not fail. In humility of mind, the meek dig down to bed-rock for the foundation of their lives. They are willing to die for the facts which are the secret of victorious living. Their irresistible power is not their own; it is the power of the deepest Reality there is, the power of God, undergirding the real.

There is, then, a second characteristic of the humble-minded. Knowing the facts and the truth about life, they can afford to be patient and serene in the face of opposition. They know inwardly that theories, opinions, and prejudices are at the mercy of the truth. A scientific theory is doomed the moment it meets one single contradictory fact. A human prejudice or an unholy opinion is likewise doomed when it meets a positive contrary fact, but it takes a longer time to get it in the grave. Opinion and prejudice drive the humble-minded to their Calvaries, but they are plagued by perpetual resurrections.

Though his observations meant a revolution in the realm of astronomy and a contest with the church, Copernicus published his book *About the Revolutions* with the confidence of one in possession of the truth. He had waited in humility for thirty-six years, testing, revising, checking his results, until he knew whereof he wrote. Let the stupid rave and rant, he could remain unmoved, knowing his truth would one day win the world.

There is abiding wisdom in the advice of Huxley to sit down before the facts "as a little child." We go wrong when we pursue conclusions without adequate seeking and finding. As Confucius put it, "Thinking without learning makes one flighty, and learning without thinking is a disaster." [10] The inward security of the meek is the fruit of knowledge and insight approving "the things that are excellent" and that "cannot be shaken and remain" [11] when the opposition has done its worst. The sovereignty of the meek comes by way of surrender to the leading of the truth. Their serenity is the bequest of their submission. The sovereign authority of Copernicus and the indestructible influence of others who searched for truth were theirs because they lost themselves in humble obedience to the truth. Meek they were, but in their meekness they baffled the mighty.

Jesus "spoke as one having authority and not as the scribes," [12] because He spoke as one who had sat down before life as a little child to read its message with humility. There is "no other way but His way" to "life that is life indeed," because the world is made the way it is and men are made the way they are. He could afford to go to the Cross and surrender His spirit to the Father in perfect trust, because He knew His way was God's way, and that men must learn it or perish. And we must learn or live to regret our stupidity, like those who seek to climb Long's Peak in Colorado without regard to the knowledge of those who know the way. Almost every summer someone is killed trying to climb the peak the

[10] Quoted from *The Importance of Living,* by Lin Yutang, John Day Co., New York, 1937, p. 364.
[11] Hebrews 12:27.
[12] Mark 1:22.

wrong way, without going through the "Key Hole," a rugged notch in the cliff just beyond the boulder field. The way to the peak is narrow but sure, and there is no other way that is safe. Not by whim or caprice does Jesus insist He is "the way," but rather because He knows the lay of the land, how the peak is made, and which trails are dead ends and which lead upward to triumph. He was "meek and lowly," yet triumphant and serene by virtue of His sublime knowledge of the facts which undergird all life and death.

A third characteristic of the humble-minded emerges from these first two. It is expressed eloquently in the answer of Michelangelo to those who sought to discredit his type of art. Said he, "I criticize by creating." The triumph of Christianity in the first three centuries came, not from embittered criticism of pagan ways, but rather from the power of creatively Christian lives, magnificently enduring the strain of combat, even when it took them to Nero's arena. The victory of democracy over ruthless authority will come in the end not by way of military triumph, not as a consequence of verbal barrages flung against their stupidity, but, rather, from the power of democracy to deal creatively and splendidly with the issues of the hour. Such is the insight of the humble-minded who follow the leading of the Master. Jesus criticized the life of His time and the ways of His ecclesiastical contemporaries by creating a way of life which has been the wonder of the world from His day to ours. By way of His creative criticism He led men to the very threshold of the kingdom until they said, "God was in Christ, reconciling the world unto himself." [13]

Go back into history, if you please, and you will see that only they who "criticize by creating" have any chance of inheriting the earth. There was that tragic time when Judah lay in ruins, her people carried into captivity. Babylon stood for power, her armies ruled the world, her kings levied tribute when and where they would. And yet, while Babylon ruled,

[13] II Corinthians 5:19.

Judah, feeling her spiritual need, sought the truth in humility and meekness. Her prophets laid hold of the moral facts in harsh experience; at least a "remnant" of her people listened in teachable thoughtfulness, and Judah created the foundations for the faith of the world. Not Babylon in her might, but Judah in her meekness inherited the earth.

Pause a moment among the shadows of history, and watch Napoleon strutting over the earth, his armies master of the continent. The timid fawned at the feet of the Corsican Corporal, risen to terrible power, and yet, as Byron understood,

> 'Tis done—but yesterday a King!
> And arm'd with Kings to strive—
> And now thou art a nameless thing:
> So abject—yet alive!
> Is this the man of thousand thrones,
> Who strew'd our earth with hostile bones,
> And can he thus survive?
> Since he, miscalled the Morning Star,
> Nor man nor field hath fallen so far.[14]

Men would have said it could not be, the mighty fallen so. While Napoleon was still strong, Germany lay in ruins at the feet of France, dejected and desolate, conquered and ruined, the hope of the Fatherland quite dead. Surely, a defeated Germany could not inherit the future. But in that hour of despair, something happened to the soul of Germany. Her philosophers and teachers began to toil with humble reverence for the truth. Kant and Hegel, Schopenhauer and Fichte awakened the world from its "dogmatic slumber." Goethe flung his poetry on a world spiritually starved, and scholars recovered the glory of the past's dead yesterdays. Surprisingly enough, it was not France with her military might that won the world; it was Germany in her defeat. She became the intellectual capital of the world, laying the benediction of her

---

[14] "Ode to Napoleon Bonaparte," by Lord Byron, from *The Poetical Works of Lord Byron*, Houghton Mifflin Co., Boston, 1880.

knowledge and scholarship on mankind. "Blessed" indeed "are the humble-minded, for they shall inherit the earth." The contrast between then and later is enough to vindicate the word of Jesus for all time. Then Germany criticized her enemies with a creativity that gave her undisputed intellectual and spiritual leadership; during the Hitler era, in seeking to criticize her enemies with violence, she wrought her doom. None but the meek ever can inherit the earth.

What is more, none but the humble-minded can be creative. George Buttrick remarks pertinently, "The mind makes its most fruitful excursions into the unknown from the base of the accepted." [15] It does not start with a vacuum, but rather from a base of knowledge achieved by patient search. No man builds bridges until he first has yielded humbly to the leading of mathematics. Humbly he must sit down before the fact that two plus two equals four and that no subtle sophistry can make it anything else. Just let him try to build a bridge on the assumption that two plus two is equal to five and you shall see how quickly the universe will devastate his pride. The scientist is humble-minded or he does not create. His experiments, wrought with painstaking care, are but evidence of his wish to be taught by the elements in his test tubes. He knows that he does not truly create, he is rather the instrument by means of which the elements of the earth discover their own possibilities. His mastery is by way of his meekness; his creativity is the testament of his humility.

Years ago I watched an artist preparing to paint the portrait of a western tanager. Watching patiently day by day near the bird's nest, he made innumerable sketches of the bird in flight, perched on a twig, feeding its little ones, scolding an unfriendly magpie. Not once did the artist strike out on his own, drawing with an egoistic imagination set free from the real. Only God could make a bird, and the artist could merely approach the final beauty of the reality before him. When at

[15] From a sermon preached at the Madison Avenue Presbyterian Church, New York City.

last the painting was finished it was lifelike in its near perfection, and yet the artist sighed as he gave the portrait to me. "No painted bird ever will capture all the beauty of the creature itself," he said. "I have painted mountains and trees and birds for many years, but they all defy my brush and colors." It was quite true, and yet his genius made him famous in the West as one who caught the color and the spirit of the mountains and the streams. His genius as a creative artist was the consequence of his humility before the realities he sought to reproduce on canvas. Without humility, there is no creativity.

"He that heareth these words of mine and doeth them, I will liken him unto a wise man that built his house upon a rock," [16] upon the abiding realities that make creative life possible. "I have one passion, it is He," is the spirit of the humble who fashion their lives in His image. They are the creators of beauty and goodness in life. With mercy and forgiveness they create "peace on earth, good will toward men." With trust and respect for persons, they create the fabric of an orderly society. With courage and sublime faith they build towers to the dignity of the human spirit to guide a wavering mankind on its way. Humbly they lose their lives "for His sake"; triumphantly they inherit the future in His name. They are critics of the commonplace by virtue of their uncommon ways. Humble before the disturbing reality of Christ, they become instruments for His creative power, and in being "lifted up" they draw men unto Him and His way. None but the meek shall create; none but the creative shall inherit the earth.

III

There is, then, a second major characteristic of meekness which goes far toward explaining both its creativity and its capacity for endurance. The word "meek" used in the gospel text is the same Greek word used by Xenophon to describe

[16] Matthew 7:24.

domesticated animals—"horses broken to bridle," or wild animals tamed and trained. Meekness is energy channeled into creative usefulness. It is the wild horse trained to use his strength for plowing a furrow, the half-wolf Alaskan husky dragging a sled over snowy wastes, the elephant moving great logs at the bidding of a man perched atop his head. It is strength and knowledge, spirit and will harnessed to creative purpose. It is disciplined power, mastered energy. No wonder Paul admonished Timothy to "follow after . . . meekness." [17]

The human spirit unbridled is a fearful thing, raging through the earth like a forest fire to destroy the fruit of centuries of growth and toil. Having "put on . . . meekness," it is like the fire under the boiler of a great steam engine, creating useful power. Our fathers overdid the matter of "total depravity," and yet they knew the reality of "rebellious flesh that would not be subdued"; they understood the flaming peril of "miserable aims that end with self." Men must be tamed, they knew, by

> . . . thoughts sublime that pierce the night like stars,
> And with their mild persistence urge man's search
> To vaster issues.[18]

There is wretchedness and waste in lives untamed, unmastered by those "vaster issues" which reach beyond the horizons of the self.

"And seeing the multitudes," distracted and distraught, anxious and troubled, haunted by their bondage to little aims, Jesus spoke to their deepest needs. He felt the futility of their feeble ways; He was disturbed by the waste of what might have been if . . . There amidst the multitudes was power to "upset the world" if He could but claim it for the Father. If the turbulence and the truculence of twisted selves could be

---

[17] I Timothy 6:11.
[18] *O May I Join The Choir Invisible,* by George Eliot, *The Oxford Book* of Victorian Verse, ed. by Arthur Quiller-Couch, Clarendon Press, Oxford, 1922, p. 330.

harnessed in the service of the kingdom, none could stand against their power. If dividedness could be turned into discipline the kingdom might be won. If, somehow, the multitudes could sense the "vaster issues" beyond their "miserable aims" and fling themselves with abandon toward the "straitened gate" and the "narrow way that leadeth unto life" the promise of the future might be won.

Quite obviously, the discipline of the meek rests back on the humble-mindedness which lays hold upon the "vaster issues" of the spiritual life reaching beyond "the huge army of the world's desires." Moses, the scriptures say, was of all men most meek, but his meekness was not born until he stood, well nigh unbelieving, before the burning bush and put off his shoes in humble reverence before the purpose of God. The undisciplined fury which killed an Egyptian slave-driver did not surrender to resolute stability until he yielded in humble submission to the gentle guidance of the spirit of God. So the humble mind, yielding to the persuasive power of issues vaster than the self, is the disciplined mind. Indeed, there can be no discipline without humility. The wild colt is not disciplined until he is humbled by a bridle and becomes submissive to its guiding. The soldier is not disciplined until he is humble before military authority, until he yields to the commands of his superiors.

Always we are disciplined by something before which we are humble. We are meek only when we bow before something transcending ourselves. Commonly, we speak of self-discipline, as if, somehow, we could put bridles on our lives and by the sheer power of the will determine the way of our going. In reality, however, self-discipline is a contradiction in terms. It is like trying to lift ourselves by our own bootstraps or guide ourselves by stars we have painted on the ceiling. Our selves are disciplined by the realities we worship, by the facts before which we are humble, by the truths that make us free. We are disciplined by the values that have mastered us, "broken to bridle" by something beyond us to which we give humble allegiance.

The golfer is humbled by the elusive little white ball he places on his tee. The ball cannot be coerced or crushed or bullied. It demands respect and deep humility. It has a stern and unrelenting discipline which it imposes on those who would follow its unaccountable goings. There are rules of stance and timing. To look up, swinging, with the eyes no longer focused on the ball, is to slice or hook or miss. Either we yield humbly to the discipline of the golf ball or we give up golf in disgust, wondering at the stupidity of those who follow its wanderings from dawn until dark. It is the humble-minded, surrendering in reverence to the ways of the golf ball who are the disciplined experts of the game.

What is more, in the process of being disciplined by the golf ball, the golfer wins a certain faith in the correct grip on his club, the right stance before the ball, and the properly timed swing. He begins to drive with assurance and effectiveness. He uses his irons with confidence and his putter with a sure touch. He has abiding faith that his shot will come out right if his stance and grip and swing and eyes are as they ought to be. That is why he stands like a prima donna in front of the ball so long trying to get set just right. His humility leads to discipline and his discipline to faith in a way that is eminently correct and right.

So it is that by way of humility constraining discipline we arrive at the unfaltering faith of the meek in a way not our way and a truth not our truth but God's. Humble before the disturbing reality of Christ, we are disciplined in a way and guided to faith in it. Beginning with the cry, "Teach me thy way, O Lord, and lead me in a plain path," [19] we yield to the discipline of "the way" and end with faith that "he that willeth to do his will, shall know" [20] that his teaching is of God. Knowing, then, by way of experience that the way is sound,

[19] Psalm 27:11.
[20] John 7:17.

we drive forward with confidence "in the power of the Spirit."

Surely, none but men of faith, sternly disciplined by their humility before the Master could have done what the Christians did throughout the first three centuries of the Christian era. No decree of the mighty could have forced the Christians to endure the catacombs of Rome. No dictator could have forced them to speak in season and out of season in Rome and Ephesus, in Athens and Corinth, in Gaul and in Spain, in the name of Christ despite peril, pain, torture, and even death. They did what they did for the sake of one who inspired their reverence, constrained their humility, lured them to harsh discipline, and led them to inflexible faith. They were disciplined by their humility and their devotion. They were struck, but they did not strike back, cursed but they did not curse; lied about, but they did not lie. They returned good for evil, mercy for brutality, forgiveness for hate. They were meek in their humility and spiritual discipline, but they were mighty, too.

Our times know no greater need than the inward discipline of the meek. "Without discipline a society, however vast its material possessions or great its membership, is helpless in the presence of crisis," says the Educational Policies Commission of the National Parent-Teacher Association. Nevertheless, education provides no dynamic for discipline unless it is Christian education, leading each "new generation of savages" to say,

> Take my life and let it be
> Consecrated, Lord, to Thee.[21]

When one is humble before Christ, inner discipline and inner control become possible; but, as Harry Emerson Fosdick insists so rightly, "no man can live an unmastered life." Either he will be mastered by low aims, unmanageable sins and unbridled passions, or he will be mastered by the Master. It will be one way or the other.

[21] From the hymn by Frances Ridley Havergal.

IV

Quite inevitably, the disciplined win out against the distracted. There is no mystery attached to this third beatitude, "Blessed are the meek: for they shall inherit the earth." Who but the humble-minded, disciplined, and reverent before some object worthy of devotion could possibily inherit the earth or anything else worth winning? Clark's description of John Keats at the table in the school dining room with a volume of Burnet's *History of His Own Times* resting on his lap for perusal is suggestive of the "narrow way" through which Keats moved to poetic power. There was a touch of the hazardous in conveying food across the open book, but there is a hint also of the disciplined passion for knowledge and humility before truth which enabled Keats to inherit the literary world of his time. He won all the available prizes and honors his school had to offer and went on to greatness. It was mental discipline wrought by his reverence for truth that did it!

The violent and the vicious, the tempestuous and the turbulent who storm through life like uncontrolled tornadoes may leave their marks of destruction upon the fair creations of the human spirit; but only the meek, whose turbulence has become tranquility are competent to build enduring monuments in heaven or on earth. It is the tranquility of training and the confidence of competence in Christ that are marks of the meek, and these are the fruit of life humble before "vaster issues" than the self. They are the issue of discipline born in the womb of reverence.

There is a sovereignty which comes by way of surrender, a serenity that is the bequest of submission. It is a paradox, but it is the secret of the meek's sure triumph on the earth. "Before I was a master, I was a slave" is a word whose truth reaches into every area of human experience. Demosthenes, a slave to a speech defect, conquered his stuttering by preaching to the sea with his mouth full of pebbles, but as he drove through the "strait gate" he drove to mastery of the art of eloquence. "Genius is nine-tenths drudgery," said President Eliot of Harvard University, with a fine appreciation of the fact that sovereignty comes by way of slavery, by way of reverence for some enduring value. The classics of art and literature, scholarship and music which have endured through time and tide are the bequest of masters who once were slaves of their ideals. No great book ever was written, no great sermon ever was preached, no worthy creation of the human spirit ever came except by way of drudgery made endurable by humble commitment to something worthy of reverence.

So great character, competent to endure the vicissitudes of fate and to deal with the tensions within the self is wrought, as Paul said, only by those who are "bond servants" of Christ. Their greatness is the greatness of disciplined goodness; their power inheres in their "mild persistence" and their undiscourageable tenacity. John Steinbeck offers a striking illustration of the conquering power of meekness in his story, *The Moon Is Down*. It is the story of what happened in a little Norwegian town when the Germans came. With neither hate nor heroics, Mr. Steinbeck suggests a creed all of us desire to maintain. "You know, Doctor," says Mayor Orden of the invaded town, "I am a little man and this is a little town, but there must be a spark in little men that can burst into flame. I am afraid, I am terribly afraid, and I thought of all the things I might do to save my life, and then that went away and sometimes now I feel a kind of exultation, as though I were bigger and better than I am."[22] It was so. John Steinbeck did not make clear, as he might have done, that the courage of Mayor Orden stemmed from the heritage of his people's faith in the righteous God. Mayor Orden, steeped in the faith of his fathers, could not run away; "a bond servant" to his ideal of integrity, he could not betray his people, and a little man in a little community became enduringly great even in death. He be-

[22] *The Moon Is Down,* by John Steinbeck, the Viking Press, New York, 1942, pp. 177-8.

came a symbol, a terrible symbol to the Germans, of the irresistible meek.

The ideals, the values, the personalities before whom we are humble become the vehicles by means of which we fulfill our destiny. They take even the little that we are and make much of it; they turn us into slaves for a while in order to make us "more than conquerors"; they defy even the cry of the spirit for self-preservation in order that the soul may be free. They make us aware of our littleness and our need that they may make us mighty with "the power of the spirit." They set us free from the tyranny of the trivial and lend us the serenity of the significant. "Blessed are the meek," humble-minded in their seeking for the truth, sovereign in their surrender to the "vaster issues" of life, disciplined by their humility before Jesus Christ, "for they shall inherit the earth."

FIVE

INTO GREEN PASTURES

THE FIRST THREE BEATITUDES HAVE TAKEN US ALONG THE ROAD of self-emptying, driving us inexorably toward dependence on the steady strength of God. Driven by our inward conflicts to an awareness of our spiritual need, and by our mourning to a deeper consciousness of the self's inadequacy, we discovered the irresistable power of humble-mindedness, reverent before values worthy of devotion. The fourth Beatitude marks the beginning of self-filling by way of dedication and commit-ment, and we enter into the green pastures of God. As we "hunger and thirst after righteousness," we are "filled" with the qualities of spirit that make the self whole.

I

Hunger and thirst are strong words and no doubt Jesus used them deliberately. Hunger is a "craving or need for food," and thirst is "a sensation of dryness with a craving for liquids." The gnawing hunger of a starved body is a terrible thing that focuses the energies of the self on the search for food. When a man is starving, nothing seems important except something to eat. He will steal or kill, beg or fight for crumbs to keep him alive. All other values become quite meaningless beside the supreme desire for food. Thirst is like unto hunger. The miner, lost in the desert and dying of thirst, will bargain all the gold he has for a single cup of cold water. Nothing is im-portant save the water that means life.

When a man is starving it is quite futile to tell him that "man shall not live by bread alone." [1] Bread is his ruling passion and his hunger for it is decisive. What he thinks, what he says, what he does are determined by his need to satisfy the craving of his body. Even cannibalism is justified in his thinking, if by devouring his fellows he can save his life. Moral values lose their significance and ideals flounder against the cutting edges of inexorable hunger.

Quite inevitably, life is organized around our most poignant hungers. Men will resort to desperate measures to satisfy a physical appetite. The dope fiend will pay any price for the narcotic he craves. No law is potent enough to stand in his way. No ideal is strong enough to thwart his quest. If steal he must, then steal he will to satisfy the perverted hunger of his body.

In the fourth Beatitude, Jesus is saying that when we want righteousness as much as we want food and drink, when we want goodness as much as we want tobacco, when the passion for integrity is like the passion of the dope fiend for a narcotic, we shall be filled. Life will be organized then around a significant and worthy hunger. When we will "walk a mile," or a second mile for the truth; when the mile seems insignificant beside the satisfaction truth yields a hungry spirit, life is organized and unified by truth. When we will "walk a mile" to make a wrong right because we are starved for righteousness, we are on the road to the fullness of life. When we will "walk a mile" to forgive someone who has hurt us because we are hungry for goodness, we are "not far from the kingdom of God." [2]

Part of our difficulty with the fourth Beatitude lies in the fact that our hungers are egocentric, independent, instinctive, accepting no unifying allegiance beyond themselves. They are of four elemental types. There are (1) second-rate hungers that demand first-rate energies; (2) there are disorganized,

[1] Matthew 4:4.
[2] Mark 12:34.

random hungers that drive us in all directions at once; (3) there is a hunger for the thing we call "life" which scatters and divides the self; and (4) there is a hunger for righteousness, for the values that abide eternally, which makes the self a whole.

Jesus speaks of the unfilled as the "lost," and there is a kindly ring to the word. No doubt He used it deliberately, as if He understood that men blunder into sin quite unintentionally because their hungers are selfish. We become lost, inwardly torn apart, divided and spiritually befuddled because we hunger most for the wrong things, because we hunger for power or wealth, or beauty or popularity and their like; because we hunger for nothing more significant than the desires of the moment; or because we hunger for happiness, or life, or pleasure. Either we give first-rate energies to second-rate hungers, or else we run hither and thither in response to the passing hungers of the moment which have no meaning beyond themselves. The first three hungers lead us into sin and lostness before we know what has happened unless they are sublimated before the altar of the fourth.

Our second-rate hungers are those that center in ourselves, demanding our best energies and contributing to our "egocentric predicament." They seem terribly important because they have their focus in us, and they lead to lostness and to spiritual poverty because they keep us in bondage to ourselves. They are, like stars painted on the ceiling of a ship's cabin, quite futile to guide us to a worthy destiny, because they shift their positions with the shifting of the ship. They take us, in the end, to nowhere worth going.

When I was a small boy, a neighborhood lad somewhat younger got lost, and the whole neighborhood turned out to search for him. Sammy was very much worth finding, and we all rejoiced when one of the neighbors found him wandering around a few blocks away. Sammy did not intend to get lost. He set out from home chasing a pretty butterfly, and the little creature led him on in all directions and then escaped. By that time, Sammy could not remember which way was home, and he became a frightened, tearful, confused little boy. Most people who get lost are very much like Sammy. They set out chasing a butterfly. It may be pride or power or passion. Catching the butterfly seems frightfully important at first, but it leads to blind alleys and dead-end streets.

Our second-rate hungers are like Sammy's butterfly—we pursue them into lostness. King Midas was chasing a butterfly when he was mastered by his hunger for gold. In the end, all the wealth that flowed from his golden touch could not atone for the dust and ashes of his soul. When he got what he wanted, he was not filled. He paid too much for too little. His daughter, turned to gold, was but a symbol of the capacity for love hardened and deadened by the second-rate hunger of his soul, a hunger that had assumed first-rate importance. It is no wonder Jesus insisted that "a man's wealth consisteth not in the things he possesseth." [3] Many a man, like Midas, has floundered into lostness, sacrificing love, integrity, mercy, kindness, and truth for the sake of a second-rate hunger for wealth. His sin is a by-product of his hunger, a consequence of commitment to a second-rate purpose. He did not intend what happened. He did not deliberately crucify the love and integrity of his spirit. They were simply the casualties of his hunger, elements of the price he paid pursuing a butterfly.

Napoleon, dedicating first-rate capacities to a second-rate hunger for power, found his power quite impotent to satisfy his spirit. He sacrificed too much to gain too little. He came to believe that "hunger, cupidity and vanity" are the motive forces of mankind because his own hunger had led him to sacrifice integrity, humility, and self-discipline. His life and his thinking were organized around his ruling passion for power, but there came a day when he sensed there had been some misunderstanding between him and heaven. His hunger was such that it could not be filled, not in God's moral universe.

[3] Luke 12:15.

John Ruskin speaks of another second-rate hunger. He calls it the "thirst for applause," [4] and it is, he says, "on the whole, the strongest influence of average humanity." Charles Dickens had it, and it led him into tragic lostness. His friendships were quite temporary, ending usually in conflict. He divorced his wife and fought with those who tried to help him. He quarreled with his collaborators and demanded his prerogatives. Stephen Leacock remarks that "an ignoramus could hurt his feelings; a fool could strike him to the heart. He must have homage; he must have recognition. Everyone, every single person, must admit that all he did was wonderful." [5] It was the homage Dickens liked, even craved, that made him a slave and turned his life into a hell on earth. Charles Dickens was not a whole, he was divided into conflicting fragments; he was not free, he was a slave.

Everywhere we turn we see men and women in bondage to their stupid, second-rate hungers. Dr. David Seabury tells the story of men who are slaves to their ambition, to their craving for power, of women who are slaves of their desire to be beautiful, or popular or accomplished. He describes one woman who came to his office after long treatment for mental disorder. At last she found freedom and later remarked: "The happiest day of my life was the day I ceased trying to be beautiful." In all probability, the hunger to be somebody causes more inward conflict and mental suffering than any other single passion of the human spirit. It destroys the wholeness of the self. It nearly wrecked the fellowship of the disciples when it caught James and John and sent them to Jesus asking for the chief seats of the kingdom. It drove Jesus to the cross when the Pharisees felt their position imperiled by the rising power of the Son of God. It left the leaders of Israel spiritually inept and inwardly tormented.

It is our selfish hungers that keep us impoverished and slaves

[4] *Sesame and Lilies,* by John Ruskin, Merrill, New York, 1891.
[5] *Charles Dickens, His Life and Work,* by Stephen Leacock, Doubleday, Doran and Company, Inc., New York, 1936, p. 31.

of dividedness. We resent what stands in our way; we are bitter in defeat; we are torn by anger when what we want is denied. We mortgage our future to keep up with the Joneses or get ahead of them if we are able. We waste our health and squander our nervous energy for a mess of pottage, and when all is said and done, we can't take it with us. It is our second-rate hungers that make us slaves, keeping us from inward health and wholeness, and leaving us quite unfilled.

II

Our disorganized, fleeting, momentary hungers are quite as devastating as our second-rate hungers. They make us their victims because no worthy hunger dominates our days. Thomas Wolfe describes a "drab and shabby street in Brooklyn," a street of cheap brick buildings, warehouses, and garages, on a Sunday afternoon in March, bleak, empty, and gray. Then he pictures a group of men hanging around on the corner in front of a cigar store. "For hours they hang around the corner, waiting, waiting, waiting—for what? Nothing, nothing at all. And that is what gives the scene its special quality of tragic loneliness, awful emptiness, and utter desolation." [6]

It is this waiting for nothing, living for nothing in particular that leaves us prey to the deceptive hungers of the moment. It fills life with sex and smut, with petty thievery and beer-parlor stupidity. Hungering for nothing in particular, we are victimized by the passing hungers of the moment. We face life like a small boy in a dime store with a quarter to spend. The boy plunges through the door all smiles and eagerness, clasping his quarter. He has not the slightest idea what he wants, but the quarter is burning his fingers. He looks at everything. There are jeeps and toy guns, whistles and pencils, comic books and balls. He wanders up and down. First he

[6] *You Can't Go Home Again,* by Thomas Wolfe, Harper and Brothers, New York, 1940, p. 429.

wants a jeep and then he wants a ball; then he changes his mind and wants a gun. The more he tries to decide what he wants, the more confused and uncertain he becomes. Finally, in a kind of desperation, he buys a whistle and he is no sooner on his way home than he is in tears because he does not really want the whistle.

Not knowing what we really want from life, we pay too much for whistles. We chase butterflies because we have nothing better to do. We choose lesser values because we have no genuine passion for something profoundly worth possessing. We get lost like the Nazis, embracing stupid creeds because we have no significant creed to guide us. We become lost in our sins because no sublime loyalty keeps us steadily on "the way." We are bewildered by "the huge army of the world's desires" because no supreme devotion guides us to sane choices and abiding values.

III

There is, then, that ineffable hunger for what we call life that leaves us, like our second-rate hungers and our disorganized hungers, quite unfilled. We pursue the illusive thing called "happiness," or life, as if "the pursuit of happiness" were the end of all living. We forget that happiness and wholeness are quite beyond the reach of our most ardent quest. "Ye shall seek me and ye shall find me if ye seek me with all your heart" [7] is by no means the promise of Pan. Seeking life or happiness or even wholeness is like plunging madly toward a mirage that fades into the horizon beyond pursuit.

Much of our wrong living is a by-product of our quest for life. We hunger for happiness, we crave the satisfaction of our desires, as if, somehow, their satisfaction would enable us to be filled. The boy who "sows his wild oats" and takes his turn at running wild and revolting against discipline is by no means just trying to establish a reputation for badness. As a

[7] Jeremiah 29:13.

matter of fact, as Dean Wicks of Princeton says, the members of the younger generation do not honestly know why they are bad or why they are good. Goodness and badness are incidental to their quest for life, by-products of their attempts to satisfy their hunger for life that satisfies. Their badness is a consequence of their suspicion that the old song is right: "You can't be good and still have any fun."

Percy Bysshe Shelley is a fine example of one who lived on the theory that goodness was too prosaic to be interesting. It really was not worth his time. When he studied chemistry at Eaton his chemical experiments were carried on not for the sake of learning, but for the sake of explosions, the bigger, the better. Once, when he was partially enveloped in a cloud of blue flame accompanying an unorthodox electrical experiment, his science teacher, Mr. Bethell, exclaimed, "What on earth are you doing, Shelley?" The quiet response was, "Please, sir, I am raising the devil." [8] He spent a large part of his life doing precisely that, not to be bad, but to find a "kick," a thrill in living.

The difficulty with our hunger for life lies in the fact that, like our second-rate hungers and our random hungers, it keeps us a prisoner of our own petty, personal wants. It sends us riding off in all directions at once. We hunger for pleasure, we crave a "kick," we cry for happiness, and we gratify the incessant desires of our bodies in the hope that we shall be filled. There is, however, a revealing word about ourselves in Michael Karpovich's recent study of Russia. He describes what he calls "the invincible stupidity" of the Russian peasant and then he remarks that he "cannot be free to do what he likes, for what he likes will keep him a slave." [9] So, our undisciplined hungers, our petty wants keep us slaves. They leave us in bondage to our inner conflicts and our inner divid-

[8] *Tuberculosis and Genius,* by Lewis J. Moorman, University of Chicago Press, Chicago, Illinois, 1940, p. 195.
[9] *Examining the Political Revolution of the USSR,* by Michael Karpovich, The New York Times Magazine Section, February 10, 1946.

edness, and cause us to be quite unfilled even when they are satisfied.

IV

Until our second-rate hungers, our random hungers, our craving for life, are brought under the discipline of our hunger for righteousness we cannot be filled. We shall starve for life until our hunger for life becomes a hunger for goodness. Inwardly we sense the truth, and yet we revolt against it. Every minister who goes to speak at colleges finds one question quite inevitable: "Why be good?" It is not asked flippantly or in jest. It is a serious and a searching question that takes us to the heart of the fourth Beatitude, "Blessed are they that hunger and thirst after righteousness: for they shall be filled." We cannot be filled, deeply satisfied without goodness. A feast of thrills quite inevitably results in psychological and spiritual famine. The world is full of folk who are "fed up" but not filled, and there is a vast difference between those states. Getting "fed up" on thrills of one sort or another is like going to a circus and feasting on peanuts, popcorn, frankfurters, and soda pop, only to suffer serious discomfort thereafter. Being filled is like the comfortable satisfaction following a dinner of beefsteak and baked potatoes. The circus type of diet begets indigestion, the other brings health and strength.

Macbeth was suffering from acute spiritual indigestion after taking a fling when he complained,

> . . . Out, out, brief candle!
> Life's but a walking shadow, a poor player
> That struts and frets his hour upon the stage
> And then is heard no more.[10]

Macbeth had been laboring under the illusion that he could force life's candle to burn with brilliance at both ends if he could gain the throne and the power of Duncan, no matter what the means. His sin, however, was like a very green apple

[10] *Macbeth,* by William Shakespeare, Act 5, Sc. 5, Line 16 ff.

which he could not digest, and in the end he discovered, as did Ahab, that his sin was greater than he could bear. Nowhere in all literature is there a more penetrating answer to the question, "Why be good?" than in Shakespeare's realistic account of the psychological and spiritual odyssey of the pretender to Duncan's throne.

Our hunger for abundant life is not satisfied by the temporary thrills afforded by our flaunting of the moral law. The moral rules of righteousness are merely instructions on how to live in the universe as God made it. To flaunt the rules is like trying to put a clock together without concern for where the pieces ought to go. Most of us in this mechanical generation have tried at some time or another to repair a clock. We usually ended by repairing it so that nobody else can repair it. We had all the parts but we did not know the rules for putting them together. We violated the nature, the character of the clock, when we broke the laws of its functioning. The clock responded by refusing to run. Sin in life is like that. It is trying to make life run by putting it together as it never was intended to be. So the answer to the question, "Why be good?" is to be found in the fact that life will not run except when it is put together as God intended it should be.

V

The very question, "Why be good?" implies doubt concerning the efficacy of righteousness as a means of self-fulfillment and wholeness. The more earnestly the question is asked, the more our "hunger and thirst after righteousness" is inhibited. That is why the third Beatitude necessarily precedes the fourth, for it is by way of humble-mindedness, of meekness, before the inexorable facts of spiritual experience that we come to trust our righteous ideals. Belief that the meek shall inherit the earth by way of their dedication to goodness and truth is basic to "hunger and thirst after righteousness." Escape from lostness demands ethical fixed points which provide

99

direction for living. Release from the sterility of spiritual poverty and inward confusion involves a conviction of the security
of our moral objectives. It was Sherlock Holmes, the master
detective created by Conan Doyle, who observed with humorous realism, "My dear Watson, you are my one fixed point in
a world of change." That grateful comment suggests the very
human need for steady stars to guide us through life's bewildering hours. Even though "time makes ancient good uncouth," [11] it remains true that we are lost without ethical fixed
points. You and I, whose hands and minds will shape the
world of tomorrow, will be blind leaders of the blind until
we have found a way of life in which we can believe; until
we hunger and thirst after a righteousness we dare to trust.
Our inward unity and stability are dependent on the assurance
with which we follow the guidance of our ethical stars. We
go down all too easily in the conflict between abiding ideals
and temporary ideologies if we lack faith in the validity of
our moral visions. The insight of Walter Lippmann is sound
when he says that those who are

> . . . all nerves and confusion and bad dreams and fears
> are exhibits produced by an age that has no central ideal
> of human life. Our task, if I may indulge in a large
> generalization, is to take part in the great task of estab-
> lishing once more some central and controlling ideals of
> human living.[12]

There is not much chance of pulling ourselves together until
we are able to say in meekness of some way of life, this is "the
way, the truth, and the life," [13] this way of righteousness leads
to security and to strength, "though the mountains be shaken
into the midst of the sea."

The trouble is, we cannot live on Main Street, "where the
race of men go by" without assuming

[11] *The Present Crisis,* from The Poetical Works of James Russell
Lowell, Vol. 1, Houghton Mifflin Co., N. Y., 1890, p. 184.
[12] Commencement address to Radcliffe College, 1937.
[13] John 14:6.

... that right is right;
That it is not good to lie;
That love is better than spite
And a neighbor than a spy.[14]

We need to know that, even when bombs are bursting in the streets of hallowed cities and tanks are rumbling down shady lanes and turning them into shambles. We may agree in moments of disgust with those who doubt that love and truth and justice are wise, but when we get down to the business of living with our neighbors and teaching our children to face life we cannot avoid assuming that moral ideals are more than arrangements of convenience. No matter how precarious our existence may be, we are under the necessity of believing that integrity is nobler than intrigue and truth better than treachery, else we are utterly lost.

We may be battered and beaten "by the bludgeonings of chance," but in the knowledge that our ideals are "a mighty fortress" against whose ramparts wrong will some day break there is a strange security and a sense of being "filled." Haldane Holstrom, an Oregon filling-station operator, struck a solid note when he said after a successful trip down the Colorado river and through the Grand Canyon in a homemade rowboat: "I knew every watertight seam in my boat. I knew the boat was sound and would hold." And then, as if it were an afterthought, he added: "You've got to know that when you run the rapids." We have to know, too, when we run life's rapids and strike its whirlpools that the values we have trusted are sound. We live by faith in our highest aspirations or we do not live at all; we flounder where the waters boil and the rocks jut out from the stream. Our doubts will never bear the burden of ourselves! Such is the essence of the word of Jesus in His parable of two men who built houses, one on the sand, the other on solid rock. When "the rains descended,

[14] *Ultima Veritas,* by Washington Gladden, from *1000 Quotable Poems,* ed. by Thomas Curtis Clark and Esther Gillespie, Willett, Clark & Co., New York, 1937, Vol. I, p. 96.

and the floods came, and the winds blew and beat upon" these houses one fell and the other stood. The wise man who built his house on the rock, Jesus said, was the man who listened to His message and believed in it, who trusted His ideals and acted on them. Come devastation or disaster, the rock would hold.

VI

Our faith in righteousness is strengthened, too, by our humble-minded discovery that in the universe as God made it, it is of the nature of evil to destroy itself, while it is of the nature of good to be self-supporting. The universe is unfriendly to the evil that men do. It defies the right of lies to live for long. What little power they have to last, still potent in the minds of men, depends on the partial truth they always seek to hide behind. The greed of men, unmastered by some hunger for the good to be attained, runs headlong into the greed of other men, and they destroy themselves in fratricidal war. What greed demands, the world denies! The things which selfishness embraces with tentacles of iron are swept away by universal laws that never change, and "the last shall be first and the first last." Unbridled force breeds ruthless force until the strong have clashed and worn each other out. The cosmos hates the wars we fight and grants no victor's crown to the winning side, but, rather, all in anguish pay the cosmic piper for their mad dances in the mood of Mars. "They that take the sword shall perish by the sword" [15] is but a way of saying that reality hates our swords and by its subtle alchemy turns their triumphs into trash.

Evil lives only by the grace of the good that is mixed together in its caldron. It is the honor among thieves which holds the thieves intact within their band. It was the half-truths, so skillfully mixed with falsehood in its propaganda, that gave the Nazi falsehood leave to rule the minds of men.

[15] Matthew 26:52.

It is because men know instinctively that there is an abiding righteousness in their cosmos which opposes evil that they seek "to make the worse appear the better part." They dignify indecency with the name of "art," until even "strip-tease" becomes respectable by the grace of "art." They "praise the Lord and pass the ammunition," as if praising the Lord removed the evil inherent in the ammunition and made war the calling of gentlemen. Take the limited good from the evil and it damns itself as if possessed, ruined by the unfriendliness of the cosmos in which it lives.

Good, on the other hand, is sustained by other goods. Truth fears no other truth as lies fear lies. Despite the protests of the stupid, a thousand truths rallied around Galileo when he found the sun to be the center of the universe. Bewildering facts fall into their places like parts of a jig-saw puzzle, each finding its explanation and its meaning in the other. The cosmos, so unfriendly to the false, sustains and gives its blessing to what is true. Love trembles not before its kind, but rather grows from more to more, embracing all within its scope. Even though

> He drew a circle that shut me out,
> Heretic, rebel, a thing to flout;
> Love and I had the wit to win,
> We drew a circle that took him in.[16]

As Edwin Markham understood, there is power in love to overcome and to embrace the world's contradictions and evils. Seeking not its own, love includes even its opposites; knowing the strength of its roots in the nature of things, "love . . . beareth all things, believeth all things, hopeth all things, endureth all things; love never faileth." [17] Hate repels and divides; love gathers unto itself all other loves. Hate smashes against barricades of its own building, destroying itself, like

---

[16] "Outwitted," from *The Shoes of Happiness and Other Poems* by Edwin Markham, Doubleday-Doran, New York, 1934, p. 2.
[17] I Corinthians 13:7.

Don Quixote, in windmills of its own making. Love creates and co-ordinates, and in its power "all things hold together," like the universe itself.

To sense the anchors of the good, to feel their strength, is to find abiding confidence in the righteous ways of Christ. It is to see that, in the long run, this is God's world and that neither our lives nor our social order can stand up in it except on His terms. Such is the insight of the righteous of the fourth Beatitude, and they are filled with sublime confidence and immortal hope, knowing that "if God be with us, who can stand against us?"

VII

When we have found the answer to the question, "Why be good?" we have taken the first step on the road to "hunger and thirst after righteousness." A sturdy faith in the validity of righteousness necessarily precedes passion for it. Nevertheless, "hunger and thirst after righteousness" is more than a matter of logical necessity. The dynamic of goodness is to be found, not in philosophy, but in love that carries us far beyond slavish obedience to negative laws. It is not mere fulfilling the letter of the law, avoiding the evil in a negative way that is vital. "Except your righteousness exceed" [18] a slavish commitment to the letter of the law, there is no fullness in the soul. It is the "second mile," [19] the forgiving "seventy times seven," [20] the goodness which is greater than the law demands, that are the essence of the righteousness of Christ. These demand something more than philosophy. It takes more than knowledge to make us good, far more than knowledge to stir us with hunger and thirst for righteousness. After studying the history of the great civilizations of the world, numerous philosophers and historians have come to the conclusion that it is no lack of knowledge that leads us to disaster after disas-

[18] Matthew 5:20.
[19] Matthew 5:41.
[20] Matthew 18:22.

ter. No, the trouble is, we do not do as well as we know! We appear somewhat like the little bad boy who listened reluctantly to the admonitions of his Sunday-school teacher and felt resentful. "Now will you be good?" the teacher concluded. "Heck, no," came the ominous reply.

Goodness goes deeper than knowledge; it has its roots in love. Guinevere, the faithless Queen of King Arthur, sensed the truth when it was too late. Tennyson makes her say:

> . . . . Ah, my God,
> What might I not have made of thy fair world,
> Had I but loved thy highest creature here?
> It was my duty to have loved the highest:
> It surely was my profit had I known,
> It would have been my pleasure had I seen.
> We needs must love the highest when we see it.[21]

It is in loving the highest that we are overwhelmed by hunger and thirst for righteousness. Like an adolescent, falling in love for the first time, we develop a passion to be as good as we can be, an abiding wish to appear at our very best for the sake of the beloved.

The truth is suggested by the story of the medieval juggler who, in his poverty and distress, was received into a monastery. He watched for a while as his monastic brothers went about serving God. They ministered to the sick with gentle skill, and sang praises and anthems with well-trained voices. They copied ancient manuscripts with patient care, and illumined the Scriptures with exquisite artistry. He could do nothing and he was deeply troubled. One night he was missed and the abbot was scandalized to find him in the chancel of the chapel, lying on his back before the high altar. There he was giving his juggling performance with every ounce of skill he possessed, keeping the metal balls aloft, throwing and spinning

[21] "Guinevere," by Alfred Tennyson, from his *Poetical Works,* Houghton, Osgood and Co., Boston, 1879, p. 211.

them with all his power and art. The abbot leaped forward
in haste and anger and voiced a rebuke for such a sacrilege,
when, so the legend goes, the statue of the Virgin moved from
the pedestal and flung her white robe over the juggler in token
that his offering—the best he had and given in love—was accepted by her Son.[22]

It is love, love for the Master who is the incarnation of all
that is good and righteous, that is the secret of our passion to
give the best we have to life; it is the key to our hunger and
thirst for righteousness, the secret of salvation from our inward dividedness. We are what we love and cherish most. If
we are not as good as the primitive Christians who won their
world, the reason is, as William Law contends, that we never
thoroughly intended to be as good as we could be. What is
more, we never really intended it, never honestly hungered
and thirsted for righteousness, because our affections were not
fixed on Christ. Our love for Him who was so courageous
that He conquered, so gentle that He touched the humblest,
so loving that He lifted the lost, and His love for us, are the
dynamic, the motive for our concern for righteousness and
truth.

VIII

But, you say, how can I love Christ? It is a question involv-
ing a paradox. You cannot love Him unless you know Him,
and you cannot know Him unless you love Him. With disturbing candor, some wag observed that most people's idea
of God is "a vague, hazy, oblong, blur," which might be said
of the average man's idea of Christ. The trouble is, we cannot love a "vague, hazy, oblong blur." We have to know anybody we love. Of course, there is such a thing as "love at first
sight," which sometimes endures after "second sight," although
that does not necessarily hold. Nevertheless, we never really

[22] *What Men Need Most,* by Hobart D. McKeehan, Fortuny's, 1940,
p. 74-5.

love anything or anybody we do not know, which is why "love at first sight" ought to wait for "second sight" before becoming too involved.

The small boy's distaste for school is the result, not of too much study, but of too little. He simply has not learned enough to love knowledge and truth. My own childhood introduction to the piano by way of weekly lessons leaves me with a sense of vast regret. I hated the piano with a malicious hatred which on one occasion tried to put the instrument out of commission. Nevertheless, my dislike for the piano was occasioned by the fact that I practiced too little to enable me to enjoy the result. In those days I did not care for the piano because I never knew enough to make real music on it, because I never really tried to become acquainted with its possibilities. It is that way with Jesus. We do not get around to loving Him because we do not know Him. Our Bibles gather dust in forgotten corners, our churchgoing is casual, our prayers are indifferent, so that our ignorance of the Master is colossal.

Every little while I hear somebody say that the most important thing in Christianity is the Golden Rule. "I try to live by that," somebody says, "and I think I am being Christian." To be sure, Jesus did teach the Golden Rule, but to assume that He taught nothing more significant, that His life and death and resurrection meant no more than a Golden Rule, which was not even original with Him, is to reveal our abysmal ignorance of Christ. Of course, we cannot love Him if we know no more of Him than that. We never shall "hunger and thirst after righteousness" until we begin to deal seriously with our spiritual illiteracy. We have to start with an act of the will which sends us out to search for knowledge of Him. Augustine started that way in the fifth century of the Christian era, and C. S. Lewis started that way in the twentieth century, and both of them ended at the same place. When they knew Jesus as He is revealed in scripture and tradition they came to love Him and to care deeply for right-eousness.

Of course, we have to go on, then, to say that we never really know Christ until we love Him. The principle holds true in all of our experience. I am amazed, sometimes, to discover the infinite capacity of a boy's mind for resisting knowledge. He can find more reasons for not learning what ought to be learned than you would imagine possible. On the other hand, he will devour a book on scouting, learn more about tying knots or making model airplanes in less time than you would believe. In one case he loves what he learns, in the other case he does not. You have to love your job to know your job. There are some people who undertake a new job and in no time they have mastered it, learned its relation to the whole of which it is a part, found ways of being more efficient. They soon become indispensable. There are others who never master their jobs or get around to understanding why things are done the way they are. The difference is that one man loves his job enough to know it, and the other man does not. So it is in all life. We never really know anybody until we have loved him deeply, for it is in love that the deepest intimacies of life are shared and confidences are given and received. After the same fashion, love for Christ begets a strange passion for knowledge of Him and a curious "hunger and thirst after righteousness."

IX

There is one further word to be said about those who hun-ger and thirst after righteousness, and it takes us back again to the corner-stone of all the Beatitudes, "Blessed are they who feel their spiritual need." Those who so hunger and thirst are acutely aware of their spiritual need. To be in love with the highest is to be aware of the gulf between our goodness and Christ's; it is to be perpetually reaching for that which is beyond our grasp, but reaching nevertheless. Anyone who thinks he is good enough does not love enough, and, in all probability, he is not good at all. Love for the highest lays demands on us and makes us aware of the urgency of our need for resources beyond the boundaries of our selves. We must know in our moral need that, as Dante says,

> So wide arms
> Hath infinite goodness, that it receives
> All who turn to it, [23]

offering "quietness and confidence" and the inward strength to stand fast in goodness.

The urgency of the inward imperative, saying "above the noise of selfish strife," "I ought, I must," demands the answer flung from the subterranean depths where "deep calleth unto deep," "I can, I will." By the grace of God I can be what God intended me to be. Indeed, it is here that we meet life's elemental hunger, the hunger for wholeness, for fulfillment. The rosebud is restless and unsatisfied until it opens into a rose, fragrant and lovely in its unfolding toward its destiny. In the quiet fields we find, as Jesus said, "first the blade, then the ear, then the full corn on the ear." Indeed, Jan Christian Smuts finds the meaning of life and God in what he calls "Holism," the principle, the power, which drives the whole of creation and all its parts toward wholeness, completeness, finishedness, toward that which God intended. Such wholeness, we have seen, is contingent upon a "hunger and thirst after righteousness" which gathers life's divided "shreds and patches" into a purposeful pattern.

In those rich moments when we are "filled," we are aware that our wholeness is more a gift of God's grace than an achievement of the self. The "hunger and thirst" which led us to feast on satisfying values came from a love that would not let us go and lured us beyond the hungers that leave life un-

[23] *The Divine Comedy*, Dante, *Purgatory*, Canto III, *Harvard Classics*, Vol. 20, P. F. Collier & Son Co., New York, 1909, p. 158.

filled. Remembering that, and the struggles of the days before we found the secret of life that is life indeed, we are constrained to be merciful toward those who are still victims of their own egos, and to face the stern demands of the fifth Beatitude.

SIX

MERCY'S FAR HORIZONS

"BLESSED ARE THE MERCIFUL" IS NOT EXACTLY A POPULAR SAYING
at a moment when the world is licking wounds inflicted by
the cruelty of mankind. We have an uneasy suspicion that
mercy and compassion are signs of weakness, afflictions of the
"tender-minded," who live in a dream world remote from
reality. We are inclined to think of our enemies in the spirit
of the woman who said concerning her faithless husband:
"I'll make him pay, and pay, and pay." It is altogether human,
this desire to teach those who have hurt us a lesson they will
not soon forget. Mercy in our times is a scarce commodity
on the market of our human lives.

Nevertheless, mercy, as Jesus saw it, is not one of life's
electives to be chosen under favorable conditions and ignored
if inconvenient or uncongenial to our mood; it is one of life's
required attitudes. The Master understood that cruelty spawns
cruelty, and hate breeds hate until the waters of life are pol-
luted to poison the spirit of men, generation after generation.
Revenge seems sweet beyond human calculation; but in the
alchemy of God it turns bitter and terrible. Punishment prepared in anger appears pleasant; but, like cider, refreshing in
its freshness, it turns into vinegar in its old age.

Jesus did not speak of mercy out of a vacuum of untroubled
life. He had seen the suffering of His own people, cursed and
crushed by their conquerors. He had felt the venom of Judah's
hate, and He knew the meaning of Judah's scheming to get
even. There was murder on dark corners as hidden daggers

flashed in the hands of the Zealots. There was slaughter in the streets as Herod struck back. There were burning villages, like Sepphoris, lighting the night skies with lurid flames, and hundreds of crosses bearing the bodies of innocent and guilty alike. Hate ruled the world that Jesus knew, hate so bitter as to defy the imagination. Roman and Jew looked at each other across a chasm of unending bitterness. No wonder the words of Jesus fell like leaden weights upon His people: "Blessed are the merciful: for they shall obtain mercy." [1] Surely no Messiah would tell a Jew to be merciful to a Roman. That was too much.

I

But was it really too much? The land dripped with the blood of Romans and Jews, and none was secure. The dirty streets of Jerusalem reeked with suspicion and intrigue, until there was no room left for peace and human trust. Little by little, "God's chosen people" were blundering into spiritual atrophy and inward death. Not thus could life go on with meaning and with hope. There were no prophets in Judah now; the soul of prophecy had perished in a deep well of hatred. There were so seers left to speak with the integrity of spiritual insight; their horizons had been blotted out by their bitterness. It is no wonder that Jesus wept over Jerusalem as He looked with deep understanding on the troubled Holy City.

The spell must be broken; that much was clear. Mercy and forgiveness were luxuries, yes, but so were hate and vindictiveness. Costly as were they all, there was a difference. Hate mortgaged the future with a debt no man ever could pay; mercy and forgiveness settled the account once and for all, and men could make a new start with the slate clean. But men are short-sighted, like Mr. Pelham, the British minister who, on being attacked in the House of Commons on the score that

[1] Matthew 5:7.

measures he proposed were merely temporary, replied, "They will last my time." After that? Well, let others deal then with the outraged colonies in America. Mercy and justice, and a permanent solution to the conflict, were too high a price to pay. Lexington and Concord and Bunker Hill were cheaper —or were they?

Again and again, we have settled the issues of conflict our own way "to last our time." "Blessed are the merciful." It is God's way of settling issues for all time, wiping the slate clean for the future, but we think the price is too high. "He talks like Jesus Christ," was the sneering comment of Clemenceau, the "Tiger of France," as he listened to Woodrow Wilson pleading for mercy at Versailles, pleading for God's way. Well, I wonder what the old "Tiger of France" would say now. I wonder what he would have thought could he but have seen his country under the Nazi heel? Would he have remembered his sneer and repented the measures "to last my time"?

Only yesterday, according to God's time, the men of power in the economic world were saying "Labor be damned." Men were cheap. They could be bought for a pittance, used until they were no longer fit for life, and then cast off like worn-out slaves. Twelve and fourteen hours a day men toiled at their machines, only to eke out an existence in poverty and squalor. Mercy, justice! Don't be silly. Only the fit and the strong were meant to survive! But what would these men of yesterday think now if they could see the legacy they left for their children? What would they think if they could know the power of those whose fathers they drove like cattle? The underdog is topdog now.

Link by link, we have forged the chain that binds us, not daring to break the vicious circle with mercy and forgiveness, not willing to wipe the slate clean for a new start. We go on and on fighting to settle things our way and to last our time, ignoring God's way and its peace for all time. Lo, the Master weeps today, not over the people of Jerusalem destroying themselves by their folly, but over the world where cities lie in ruins and little children weep and are afraid. "Blessed are the merciful: for they shall obtain mercy."

II

Shall there be no judgment, then, no issues drawn between the right and wrong? Shall we forgive and forget with sentimental indifference to the hurts and the wounds inflicted by the cruel? Shall we make it easy for the evil to be strong again? Not if we have our wits and our good sense about us. Mercy implies no lack of judgment, no failure to condemn the wrong; but mercy is judgment in love, it is condemnation in compassion. If we have good sense, we judge our children. We condemn their wrongdoing and now and then inflict just punishment. We have no wish to make easy a repetition of their wrong. But we judge them in love, with mercy. Have you ever noticed the difference in effect between a spanking administered in the heat of an angry passion and a spanking administered reluctantly in love, even with the words, "This hurts me more than it hurts you"? I suppose the spanking feels the same to the recipient of it regardless of the mood in which it is administered. Nevertheless, the effect is quite different. In the former case its consequence is a frozen, bitter spirit; in the latter, a contrite, yielding spirit. The spanking administered in the fury of anger increases misunderstanding and antagonism; a spanking administered in love begets a deeper trust, a feeling of being judged by a standard more objective than a momentary passion.

Quite obviously, the punishment we inflict on our children is designed to cure their misbehavior, and it does no good whatever unless the children know they got only what they had coming to them. That is to say, their punishment was impartially just, the inevitable retribution for wrong. Such just punishment administered in love, is creative, even redemptive, in its results. Indeed, there is a bit of sound wisdom in the song of Koko in the *Mikado,* wherein he sings soberly, "Let the punishment fit the crime." However, as Socrates understood, sheer justice in human relations is no easy matter. Justice may be a weasel word with a very slippery meaning. The difficulty with just judgment lies in the fact that our feelings, our hurts, our prejudices and our fears, all are ingredients composing our judgments. In courts of law even impartial judges find the administration of justice a precarious business. The five to four decisions of the United States Supreme Court and the court's reversal of itself on more than one occasion suggest that justice usually is biased by the feelings and the philosophy of those who judge.

When it comes to judging our enemies in the arena of world affairs the problem of doing justly is intensified a thousand-fold. There is no impartial judge to mediate between the nations or to assess the guilt of all who helped to make the world the way it is. There are only those who struggle for advantage, one sorely wounded by the other. There is no authority beyond the will of contestants for power; and might, even though it be in the hands of the idealists, does not insure the right. Even men of integrity and good will are often biased by their frustration, their pain and suffering, so that sheer justice in judgment is incredibly difficult. It may be, then, that Browning's generally unlovely character, Bishop Bloughram, had it right when he said to a young man:

> The common problem, yours, mine, everyone's
> Is not to fancy what were fair in life,
> Provided it could be—but, finding first
> What may be, then find out how to make it fair
> Up to our means; a very difficult thing. [2]

So, if perfect justice is beyond the scope of human thought, better yet is mercy—judgment in love—capable of guiding our enemies to a better way of life and thought. Judgment in love

[2] "Bishop Bloughram's Apology," by Robert Browning, *Complete Poetical Works,* Houghton, Mifflin Co., Boston, 1895, p. 350.

has a redemptive quality in it, rebuking the sterility of cold justice.

Ignazio Silone, the Italian novelist, has described what happened to some of his friends who were ground with wars, with revolution and fascism, and through their suffering and hurt came upon a great discovery. "One should act toward others," he said, "as one would like to have them act toward one's self." The discovery, not altogether new, seemed quite astonishing to one who had come on it by way of harsh and terrible experience. It had not come second-hand from a book, but first-hand from life itself. Out of the turbulence of human struggle a poor, hurt, troubled soul blundered into the startling discovery that his enemies could be, would be, his friends if he but caught the spirit of the ancient wisdom of God. The merciful, he came to see, would obtain mercy and friendship: the merciful might redeem even the cruel.

Mercy is judgment in love that seeks to make our enemies our friends. Mercy is dealing with our enemies as we would wish them to deal with us if we were in their shoes. Abraham Lincoln asked an irate senator who was intent upon grim punishment for the South: "Do I not overcome my enemy if I make him my friend?"

III

Oh, I know that our deepest instincts and feelings often run against the current of mercy and forgiveness. But it is a case of the spirit of God against the spirit of man, and once again we face, as face we must, our spiritual need. Henry Thoreau had it right long ago when he noted that if a man is marching out of step, struggling against the current of his time, it is because "he hears a different drummer." He goes on to say, "Let him step to the music which he hears." [3] He can do no other. If he hears the music of the spirit, often "measured and far away," he will hearken to the cry for mercy and for-

[3] *American Renaissance,* F. O. Matthiessen, Oxford University Press, New York, 1941, p. 84.

giveness. Christ is a "different drummer" bidding men be out
of step when hate is rife within the souls of men. He stands
like a veteran of the ages, speaking with the voice of eternal
wisdom from His own cross, "Father, forgive them, they
know not what they do." [4] He speaks, and in His words we
hear the voice of God blowing like a gentle wind across the
tortured earth. "His mercy endureth forever," [5] despite our
disobedience, despite our rebellion against His will, despite
our wilful perversity. Indeed,

> The quality of mercy is not strain'd,
> It droppeth as the gentle dew from heaven
> Upon the place beneath. It is twice bless'd:
> It blesses him that gives and him that takes.
> 'Tis mightiest in the mightiest.
>
> .   .   .   .
>
> It is an attribute of God Himself;
> And earthly power doth then show likest God's,
> When mercy seasons justice. [6]

It is this "attribute of God Himself" which stands out so
clearly in the portrait of God painted with spiritual beauty
and tenderness in the words and ways of Jesus. Lost though
we may be in sin and evil, He would forever "seek and save
that which is lost." [7] He "seeth in secret," [8] "knoweth your
hearts"; [9] reaches out in love to the leper and the outcast, to
the hurt and the wounded. Even the "lilies of the field" are
the concern of the Father, who likewise knows the birds as
they nest. God cares for them; how much more will He care
for you. "Ye are of more value than many sparrows." [10] Here
is pictured for us all the spirit of a Compassionate Goodness

---

[4] Luke 23:34.
[5] Psalm 136:1. The phrase is repeated forty-two times, as a recurring
refrain in the Old Testament.
[6] *The Merchant of Venice,* by William Shakespeare, Act IV, Sc. 1.
[7] Luke 19:10.
[8] Matthew 6:4.
[9] Luke 16:15.
[10] Luke 12:7.

at the heart of our universe. Here is love that cares, that forgives and redeems.

We rise no higher than the God we worship and win no values richer than the ones we see in Him. Our love for others is but the shadow of His love, our mercy but the dim reflection of the everlasting mercy of the Father. If we "forgive those who have trespassed against us," it is because we have prayed "forgive us our trespasses," with simple trust in God's mercy. If we go on believing in the "ultimate decency" of those who have fallen, and whose indecencies have hurt us, it is because we know the love of God has followed us even in our falling. "Dearly, dearly 'hath he loved," and by His love we have been lifted to dignity beyond our own. To turn from mercy and forgiveness is to confess our lack of faith in God; it is to say that we no longer trust His way.

God's mercy hinges on His faith that men can come to be themselves in answer to unfailing love. So His love endures, believing in us even when we have lost faith in ourselves. He does for us what we could not do for ourselves. Despite our sins and failures, He gives us back our self-respect. See Him believing still in the Prodigal Son, even when the lad had fallen to the level of "eating the husks that the swine did eat," sure that in the end he would come to himself and return to the Father's house. Watch Him dealing with the dismal Zacheus, discovering possibilities of fineness of which even the dishonest man himself was unaware. Who, save God, was there left to believe in the demoniac who made his home among the caves by the sea of Galilee? Who but God would trust the virtue of the woman taken in adultery and send her home forgiven, with the confident admonition, "Go and sin no more"? [11] How absurd it seemed to believe in the impetuous Peter and call him "this rock," [12] when his ways suggested, not solidity and courage, but weakness and the instability of the shifting desert sands.

[11] John 8:11.
[12] Matthew 16:18.

There is an astonishing insight into the heart of God in the dramatic scene in A. J. Cronin's *Keys of the Kingdom,* where the agnostic Dr. Tulloch lies dying after a life unimpressed by the claims of religion. "I still can't believe in God," says the stricken man in his last breath. Father Chizzom replies, with great gentleness, "Does that matter now? . . . He believes in you!" [13] Even when the sons of men strive with one another like beasts of the field "his mercy endureth." He still believes in what we can be and in mercy and compassion waits to claim it. He stands at the door, knocking even though we have resolutely closed the door upon Him. The divine initiative is as constant as the stars, as inescapable as the moral law within. It seeks us out through strain and stress, in calm and in storm, knowing that what we have been is no measure of what we can be when the gates of the heart are open to receive the Holy Spirit. It is as H. Wheeler Robinson says,

> . . . in spite of our sins, the Holy Spirit does not abandon us. He remains to reinforce the voice of conscience, to awaken the slumbering spark of higher aspiration into a clear flame, to bear with us the shame of our broken vow and frequent fall.[14]

Even at the human level the power of love that mercifully believes in us in spite of our failures and our sins is one of the most potent sources of redemption we know. Many a young man has been saved from the worst in himself by the mercy of a mother or a father who refused to believe he was as bad as he seemed to be. He may not be all his mother thinks he is, but her love constrains him to be better. Long ago, we might well have surrendered to our moral defeats and failures save for the faith and the confidence of another's love. Who can measure the influence of Barnabas and his sure faith in

[13] *The Keys of the Kingdom,* by A. J. Cronin, Little, Brown & Co., New York, p. 211-12.
[14] *Redemption and Revelation,* by H. W. Robinson, Harper & Bros., New York, 1942, p. 294.

what John Mark could become? My own father taught me the meaning of redemptive love, even though he was unaware of what he did. It was in the days when I was the reluctant piano pupil of an aspiring teacher who felt it necessary to exhibit her skill by occasional recitals given by her pupils. I had prepared for one of these frightening exhibitions religiously if reluctantly. Two others performed before it was my turn. Mounting the stage, I sat down at the piano, only to discover I did not remember how to begin. I was to have played half a dozen chords moving on then to a little selection called "Moonlight on the Water." In desperation I sat until the silence was ominous. The chord I finally struck had no relation to the pleasing notes that should have come from the piano. My second effort was another painful discord. I glanced up at my family. Father was sitting silently glum, biting his lips; mother was blushing furiously, and my sister was laughing. After several false starts, I concluded "Moonlight on the Water" and sat down to a smattering of polite applause. On the way home little was said, but as I got out of the car, my father put his arm around me and said, "Son, I know how you feel, but never mind. You and I know you can play those chords and 'Moonlight on the Water,' and so long as we know it what do we care about anybody else?" That was salvation from despair to me. In spite of my failure and his embarrassment, my father still believed in me. Enrich that experience a thousandfold and you will come to understand that, in spite of failure and defeat, it is God who goes on believing in you, not merely a human father, and that the redemption involved is utterly sublime.

What faith in the merciful redeeming love of God can mean to a generation whose confidence in humanity is at low ebb and whose cynicism is a by-word is incalculable. If we are to build wisely from the wreckage of the present we shall need to believe in ourselves again because we know God believes in us too. The pagan ideologies of our time have said all too eloquently that we were not able to bear the burden of ourselves when our faith in God gave way under the staggering impact of a materialism which in its pride committed redeeming love into the hands of the simple-minded. It never was more difficult to believe in ourselves and in our fellowmen than it is today when the worst in men is being flaunted for the world to see. We must know, if we would save ourselves, that there is mercy at the heart of things still believing in men; still certain the past has not as yet revealed what we can make of ourselves and our world. As John said, "It doth not yet appear what we shall be" [15] when we truly become sons of God, responding to His perpetual divine initiative. Here is the only foundation there is for man's mercy to man. It is the faith of God that men can be reclaimed from their lostness. No man can cease from mercy when he knows what love can do! No man can surrender to the vengeful spirit if his anchors are in the heart of God.

IV

The quality of mercy that is "an attribute of God Himself" is suggested not only in redeeming love, but also in the forgiving love which is revealed so clearly in the personality of the Master. "Father, forgive them, they know not what they do" [16] spoken from the cross, is the ultimate in forgiving love. It sounds a note which goes beyond what we find in history and nature, where we see inexorable laws at work. There sin brings retribution as sure as the coming of the dawn, and evil leaves its sordid trail of suffering and anguish in human history. Sowing the wind, we reap the whirlwind, and if we dance to sensuous tunes we pay the piper in the end, whether we like it or not. There is no forgiveness in nature, where abuse of the body brings inevitable destruction and decay. There is no forgiveness in history, wherein defiance of the laws of God yields broken lives and disorder in civilized

[15] I John 3:2.
[16] Luke 23:34.

life. "Forgive us our trespasses" [17] is a prayer whose meaning hinges on a view of God which stems only from the mind of Christ. Unless there be a Christlike God we pray in vain to be forgiven for our sins.

Yet, be forgiven we must if we would live at peace with ourselves and win the satisfaction of a life made whole. It is not that forgiveness writes off the consequences of our sins and avoids our payment of their price. Retribution is inexorable! We are punished by our sins, forgiveness or no forgiveness. Punishment, however, is bearable when it has been redeemed by the grace of forgiveness. It is alienation from the sinned-against and the loneliness of bitterness that leave us broken by the evil things we have done. To lose our sense of belonging to the commonwealth of God is the cruelest aspect of our punishment for sin. To know there is a barrier between ourselves and God is to suffer the deepest anguish human life can know. We may miss the theological implications of our inward discontent and hence seek relief in wrong directions. Our lives may be at sixes and sevens, inwardly torn by remorse and regret, driving us blindly to seek secular means of escape, when, in reality, only faith in the forgiveness and the love of God can help us. "Mother, I don't mind being spanked," said a small boy, "but please don't look at me that way." Such is the voice of our deepest experience. We can endure sin's punishment; we cannot endure the alienated state of being unforgiven.

Faith in the fact of forgiveness is a basic necessity in the recovery of the self's unity. The moral failure implicit in human sin involves defiance of the inward imperatives we know we must heed in order to live at peace with ourselves. To be unable to fulfill the demands of our own imperatives is to find our self-esteem undercut, our pride dangerously deflated, our need for mercy great. Much depends on the way we choose to restore our self-respect. On the one hand, we may

[17] Matthew 6:12.

choose the way of Browning's Ottima, and wish to be "magnificent in sin," as if the very daring of our moral defiance were evidence of our self-confidence and our adventurous pride. Indeed, the Nazi program as announced in *Mein Kampf* and in the official Nazi propaganda suggested an attempt to recover self-respect by being "magnificent in sin." There is evidence to suggest Nazi pride in doing what was shockingly unmoral. Clearly, this way of restoring self-respect either to an individual or nation leads to disaster.

On the other hand, there is the way of mercy and forgiveness which relieves men and nations of the necessity of daring persistent pursuit of sin as a way of escape. To hear God saying to our sin-troubled hearts as He said to the woman taken in adultery: "Neither do I condemn thee: go thy way; from henceforth sin no more" [18] is to belong again, to end the sense of alienation from the good and be at peace with ourselves. The good news that God forgives is news of tremendous consequence for men and nations caught in the toils of their sins and not yet daring to seek peace and security in the forgiveness of the living God. We have yet to learn that God is not only love; but God is forgiveness, too. Such is the word of Jesus.

The forgiving mercy of God revealed in Jesus Christ lays the foundation for the constructive rebuilding of life unspoiled by bitterness and undistorted by the sense of lostness, of not belonging. Under the impact of forgiveness there is a mellowing of spirit rather than the hardening of spirit experienced by the unforgiven. Sin becomes not an impossible obstacle, but a means of grace. Punishment is transformed into insight, faith, and spiritual experience, because there is neither resentment nor anger in it. Suffering is seen as justice, but justice tempered with mercy and utterly without vindictiveness. Pain becomes a discipline to be endured for the sake of redemption and release, not a vengeance to be resented. The consequences

---

[18] John 8:11.

of sin remain, but they are amazingly altered and reinterpreted in the light of God's forgiveness. They are dignified and enriched with meaning which halves their hurt: "Blessed are the merciful: for they shall obtain mercy."

The significance for our world of the forgiving initiative of God reflected in the prayer, "Forgive us our trespasses, as we forgive those who trespass against us," cannot be overestimated. It implies an obligation to forgive with an openhandedness akin to that of God. It demands a spirit with neither hate nor vindictiveness as the base for both social security and spiritual serenity. It lifts a warning hand against hatred, bitterness, and a vindictive spirit. Not hatred, but forgiveness is the key to future peace and to security as well, as Madame Chiang Kai-Shek has affirmed repeatedly. While she and her people were enduring the ravages of Japanese invasion and ruthlessness, she urged the necessity of forgiveness for the enemy, in an address at Madison Square Garden, because, she said, "There must be no bitterness in the reconstructed world. No matter what we have undergone and suffered, we must try to forgive those who injured us and remember only the lesson gained thereby."

It is the ravaged and the hurt who must find it in their hearts to forgive, for only those who are calm, poised and open-minded, only those who are able to forgive such as have trespassed against them will be fit to build a world more decent and more noble in the generations yet to be. They alone can save the world from the tragedy of vindictiveness, saving the defeated from the will to regain their "face" with new magnificence in sin. Understanding that God is forgiveness, they will restore the shattered self-esteem of their enemies with the dignity and the grace of forgiveness. We dare not again defy the very nature of God in the reconstruction of the world. We are impelled to go with, not against, the spirit of God or we shall perish by our own stupidity.

Our forgiveness of those who have hurt us may well follow the conclusion that in truth all of us stand in need of the forgiveness of God. The burden of guilt weighing upon the men and women of our generation, involved in the sin of war, emotional participants in its mass hatred, personally involved somehow in the starvation of little children and the bombing of hallowed cities, deeply engulfed in the moral sag of the times, creates a desperate need for the forgiveness of the Father. Either we will find forgiveness in the love of God, or we will retreat into cynicism, bitterness and frustration. We will find forgiveness or we will lose the peace and spoil our dream; for a better world cannot be built on the bitterness of souls tortured by their sense of guilt. The disposition which after the First World War wrote into the Treaty of Versailles a clause asserting the "sole guilt" of Germany was an attempt on the part of the Allies to escape the haunting sense of common guilt, and the rise of Nazi power was, at least in part, a consequence of the German will to deny the "sole guilt" accusation. The widespread cynicism which engulfed the world in the 20's was the penalty of our spiritual failure, for we sought not forgiveness, but escape. We found neither! Our hope now lies in our response to the forgiving initiative of God, the Father of our Lord Jesus Christ. Without the consciousness of forgiveness and mercy we cannot build enduringly. "Blessed are the merciful" who have known the mercy of God.

V

Perhaps such merciful redemption and forgiveness seem too easy, but when we sense the meaning of the cross their cost to God is clear. If the cross says anything, it is that the mercy of the Father finds its triumph by way of suffering love. God is no casual giver of grace, no indifferent patron of tortured conscience. Dr. William Henry Boddy sensed the truth when he said in a sermon preached during the First World War:

Where is God today when armies clash in deadly battle? God is where mercy binds a wound; God is where sympathy stoops to share the awful burden; God is where grief sheds a tear and a little song of hope and love is at the heart of the battle's hell. God, I am sure, is where tired, brave, bewildered lads lie down to die with forgiveness in their hearts. Aye, wherever the Cross is, God is there, hanging upon it.[19]

Mercy is meaningless from one who has not suffered, paid dearly for the right to forgive. The God who stands revealed by the Cross of Christ is love that suffers in our suffering, and feels the anguish of our hurt. "Behold, the Lamb of God that taketh away the sin of the world" [20] is a figurative way of saying that in suffering love God wins the right to forgive, to take away the sin of the world.

At the very beginning of His ministry, Jesus interpreted His Messiahship in terms of the Suffering Servant of Isaiah. In all probability that interpretation is implicit in His baptism. Certainly it became explicit when Peter's great confession at Cæsarea Philippi acknowledged Him to be the Messiah. Thereafter He persistently pointed His disciples toward Himself as a suffering Messiah, and through Himself to the suffering of his Father. There is abiding truth in the story told, I think, by G. Studdert-Kennedy, to whom the suffering of God on the battlefield was as real and far more comprehensive than the suffering of the wounded and the dying. "What I want to know, Padre, is, what is God like? I never thought much about it before the war. But now it all seems different," said a wounded British officer. "When I am transferred to a new battalion, I want to know what the Colonel is like. He bosses the show, and it makes a lot of difference to me what sort he is. I realize now that I'm in the battalion of humanity, and I want to know what the Colonel of the world is like. That is your business, Padre, you ought to know." For answer the Padre pointed to the image of Jesus on the Cross

[19] From a sermon preached at the First Presbyterian Church of Chicago, Illinois.
[20] John 1:29.

which hung on the wall and both were silent, looking at the battered, wounded, bleeding figure, nailed to a cross, helpless, defeated by the world, broken in all but spirit. After a while the officer said, "God like that, Padre? No, no, God is almighty, ruler of the world, king of kings. Jesus is splendid— He is like my friends at the front, sublime in courage, His patience, His unbroken spirit. But tell me what God is like." "Yes, God is like that," the Padre answered, pointing again to the great sufferer. "Jesus was weary, hungry, tortured, crucified, and He said,

'He that hath seen me hath seen the Father.'

We have made an awful mistake about God, my friend. He is not far off behind the mists of the Milky Way; He is here; He suffers in and with the sufferings of humanity. 'This is my body, broken for you.'" [21]

So God suffers with us and in sharing our woes and the tragic consequences of our sins wins for us the right to mercy and forgiveness. God suffers when men thwart the realization of His aspirations for the world by their persistence in evil ways. God suffers when the children of His creation suffer as the result of the sins which so easily beset them. He is no idle dreamer of the skies, but is "nearer than hands and feet," traveling the trails of the world beside us, walking through the "valley of the shadow" and holding our hands, journeying with us to the ends of the earth when war flings its burden on humanity's spirit. In suffering love He goes with us to forgive and gloriously to reclaim that we may enter into the gates of the larger life.

It should be noted, finally, that it is through the suffering love and mercy of God that the sin of man is transformed into redemptive power. Human life knows no more potent force for good than love which suffers for our sins. We cannot escape it nor can we defy it; it breaks down the stoutest bar-

[21] I regret I am unable to trace the source of this story.

riers we build against it, and constrains us to some nobility. Says a suffering woman to her erring husband, "We will face this thing together, you and I, until we win over it." Such love, breathing "the attribute of God Himself," is more than any man can bear. It becomes for him a sacred grace, inspiring repentance and reform. Enrich such love a thousandfold until it becomes the love of God poured out on a cross for the sake of all of us—love which says in its agony, "We will face this thing together, you and I, until we win over it"—and you possess the power to break the tyranny of any sin. So it is that God enters creatively with mercy into the fellowship of human suffering, transforming sin into a means of grace and power.

We shall need such grace and such power if we are to deal positively and creatively with the issues of our times and with the sins which have brought us where we are today. The future belongs to the merciful who have known the mercy of God! What is more, having known the mercy of God, the merciful are constrained to be pure in heart, that they may see the God whose mercy they have known.

—⸱❧{ SEVEN }❧⸱—

GOD ON OUR STREET

THE SOLDIER OF THE FIRST WORLD WAR WHO SAID TO BISHOP McDowell just before going "over the top," "What do you know about God? Quick!" expressed a universal longing. That yearning for knowledge about God has flung itself like an echo from age to age. "O that I knew where I might find him, that I might come even to his seat" is a cry that is as old as man. Philosophers and scientists, poets and prophets, mystics and men of the world all have tried their hands at describing the character of God. The child's eager urging, "Tell me something about God," has its roots in psychological and spiritual necessity as Philip understood when he said, "Lord, show us the Father, and it is enough." [1]

It is not merely knowledge about God that we seek. The theologian is not satisfied with meticulous definition and the philosopher is not content with logical speculation. Shelley put his finger on the crux of the matter when, in his preface to "Alastor," he suggested the profound dissatisfaction of a young man who sought beyond the wonder and the beauty of the external world for intercourse "with an intelligence similar to himself." We want something more than "ghostly voices" speaking from the musty pages of our many books. Ours is

> . . . unfaith clamouring to be coined
> To faith by proof,[2]

[1] John 14:8.
[2] *Earth and Man*, by George Meredith, from *The Poetical Works of George Meredith*, Charles Scribner's Sons, New York, 1912, p. 245, St. 41.

129

proof that comes by way of spiritual experience. We would move with Job from saying "I had heard of thee by the hearing of the ear," to the deeper word, "but now mine eye seeth thee." [3]

Jesus spent His life and His ministry trying to "show us the Father," to enable us through the eyes of faith to know what God is like and to share His sublime comradeship. By way of Jesus Christ we have seen the love, mercy and forgiveness of the Father, and through the Master we have come to know that these qualities of spirit in ourselves are evidence of God's immanence in the human spirit. Our task now goes deeper than a portrait of God; it is to achieve an experience of God. Perhaps the word "achieve" puts the emphasis too much on us and not enough on the grace of God. Nevertheless, "to see God" is both achievement and gift. The achievement lies in the competence to accept the gift, to recognize it for what it is.

Many a man has stood in the presence of God without knowing it. It was so with Moses, who did not know until he was told that "the place whereon thou standest is holy ground." [4] It was thus with Jacob, who awakened from a dream-laden sleep to say, "Surely the Lord is in this place, and I knew it not. This is none other than the house of God, and this is the gate of heaven." [5] It was then that he wrestled with his own soul and God "until the breaking of the day," transforming his spiritual poverty into a final assurance.

I

We who have sensed our spiritual need and understood our futility without God have come humbly on the fifth Beatitude in the knowledge that here is the spiritual key to man's vision and knowledge of God. "Blessed are the pure in heart: for

[3] Job 42:5.
[4] Exodus 3:5.
[5] Genesis 28:17.

they shall see God." [6] Instinctively we have known that only the pure in heart ever could see God or feel the benediction of His peace. Only the pure can know the pure. We have no comradeship except with those who share our likes. Oil has no fellowship with water, for the two are separated by natures so different as to defy each other. Neither can cross the threshold of the other's life; each dwells in its separate zone. There are men whose lives we cannot invade with fellowship. Their faiths and their philosophies, their "love of sinning," and their hardened ways create a gulf we cannot breach unless there be a change in them or us. So there are men God cannot reach, their very impurity constituting a barrier His purity cannot cross, their hardness repelling His great goodness. It is the pure, whose very purity is an invitation to the purity of God, who know even as they are known.

Quite inevitably, Christ's promise to "the pure in heart" comes after His invitation to "hunger and thirst after righteousness," and after His admonition to mercy and forgiveness. Such is the logic of all experience. Righteousness, "hunger and thirst" for goodness, which includes mercy and forgiveness, necessarily precedes spiritual vision. There can be no insight into reality until there is integrity of intention and motive. We cannot find ourselves in God until we have lost our lives for Christ's sake and captured something of His spirit in our lives. We were created for fellowship with the Father, but that fellowship is an unfulfilled hope until we are "the new creation" God intended us to be.

The very phrase, "the pure in heart," suggests integrity of being. The word "pure" implies the absence of impurity: a virtue which advertisers are sure to announce as a means of praising their products. Pure Vermont maple syrup is a palatable edible to be prized. It is not watered, nor mixed with anything else. It is the real thing. Pure gold is gold unadulterated by alloys, and pure tone is perfect tone, unspoiled by

[6] Matthew 5:8.

harshness or by shades of other tones. In short, a thing is pure when it actually is precisely and only what it is supposed to be. Canned foods are prepared in accordance with federal pure food laws, so that when you buy a can of corn or peas you can be certain that the contents of the container are one hundred per cent as represented on the label. So, being "pure in heart" is being what we are supposed to be; it is living up to the label "made in the image of God." It is all very well to suggest, as does Horatio Hackett Newman, that man is "an aqueous solution of proteins seasoned with a dressing composed of ever varying amounts of oil, sugar and salts of various kinds," [7] provided we go on from there to the spiritual realities which undergird the sacredness of the human soul. As Shakespeare put it,

> I am but the shadow of myself
> My substance is not here,
> For what you see is but the smallest part
> And least proportion of humanity.[8]

The tragedy of so much of contemporary life lies in the fact that men live as if "the least proportion of humanity" were the whole. A large number of our modern novels were written on the assumption that man is merely an animal with glands to be exercised and desires to be satisfied. So it is that the characters who live in print seldom live up to the label "made in the image of God." Not often do they get around to being what they were intended to be.

Unhappily, it requires more than the shadow of ourselves to live; it takes the "substance." You cannot make music on a piano with half the strings gone; you cannot enjoy driving an automobile with half the spark plugs fouled; you cannot paint pictures with nothing but oil, you have to have pigment too. No more can we live without the substance of the soul,

[7] *The World and Man,* Edited by Forest Ray Moulton, Literary Guild, New York, 1937, p. 196.
[8] *Henry V,* Part I, Sc. II, Line 3.

the part that is made "in the image of God," [9] to "hunger and thirst after righteousness" and to "love mercy." Man is not man until he becomes what he is supposed to be. Yea, "the whole world travaileth and groans—labors in birth pangs—awaiting the emergence of the children of God." [10] In anguish and anxiety our world waits for men to be men, wrought anew "in the image of God." "Blessed are the pure in heart," the men and the women who by the grace of God have become what they are supposed to be.

II

Percy Ainsworth suggests with pertinent insight that "the things we miss seeing are the things we miss being." [11] The naturalist, simply because he is a naturalist, sees in nature what the ordinary man does not see. The chemist, because he is a chemist, sees in the elements possibilities and powers which the rest of us miss. His seeing is contingent on his being. The pure in heart see God because they are pure in heart. Their insight is a consequence of their being what they are.

Being is "conscious existence"; it is awareness, the capacity to respond to reality. Growth in being is a matter of enlarging our capacity for response to the rich variety of realities around us. It is the cultivation of our sensitivity to the values hidden in the universe. When Jesus told Nicodemus he must be "born again" [12] in order to enter "the kingdom of heaven" He meant to suggest that Nicodemus must become aware of a reality as yet beyond the scope of his experience. Even though Nicodemus was a leader of the Jews, he still had a spiritual "blind spot," which Jesus wished to transform into under-standing. Indeed, life is a process of eliminating our blind

[9] Genesis 1:27.
[10] Romans 8:22.
[11] *The Heart of Happiness,* by Percy C. Ainsworth, Fleming H. Revell Co., New York, p. 120.
[12] John 3:3.

spots and emerging into new areas of awareness and being. It is a perpetual process of rebirth. The newly-born infant is merely a bundle of unorganized possibilities, kicking and squirming his way into "the blooming, buzzing confusion" of the world. He is in a state of suspension, born and yet not born; born into the physical world, not born into the world of meaning and value. He is little more than a stomach to be fed, a collection of unorganized desires to be satisfied. At the outset, the baby is in reality merely "the least proportion of humanity." Day by day, however, he achieves "the substance" of himself as he is born into successive worlds. In the process of becoming something, he "sees" more and more.

As times goes on, the child emerges into the realm of language, wherein unintelligible sounds become identified with things. The child is introduced to the miracle of words and sentences by means of which ideas are shared and wants made known. To be sure, the lips may fumble and the tongue may twist, so that the early language of the child is understood only with difficulty, but there is a sure movement toward meaning. With new birth into the world of language there is a kindling of curiosity and there are endless questions to be answered. Indeed, birth into the world of language is one indispensable key to his knowledge, wisdom and insight. He must be born into the realm of language, into a new area of being, in order to "see" the world.

One day, quite unknowing, the child runs headlong into the world of moral values, wherein right is right and wrong is wrong. It is a world in which truth-telling is important and lies are not tolerated; kicking, biting, and scratching have no place in this new world of ethical dignity. There is likely to be resistance to emergence into moral ways, birth pangs, if you please; and yet there can be no moving on to larger insight apart from the growing pain of rebirth into this new area of being. It is the "narrow way," beyond which lies experience in the realm of the spirit.

It is by a process of rebirth that the child achieves an appreciation of esthetic values, too. The flower, hitherto something to be bereft of its petals, becomes a thing of beauty. The sunset, once passed by with unseeing indifference, becomes a wonder to behold with rapture. "The heavens declare the glory of God" for the first time, "and the firmament showeth his handiwork" with a splendor never sensed before. Life takes on new richness and new glory; the soul adds a new dimension to "the substance" of itself and a new capacity to see God.

There is no end to the succession of worlds into which we may be "born again." History, science, poetry, literature, mechanics, law, each has its separate realm. Each remains a mystery until we emerge out of darkness and into its light. The tart observation of the late Henry Ford that "history is bunk" is no reflection on history. It suggests, rather, that Mr. Ford had yet to be born into the realm of history, vast in movement and meaning. My mystification when the scientist tells me that the table on which I write is composed of billions of electrons and protons playing leap-frog with one another is no reflection on the scientist. It merely says that I have yet to be born into the world of science. Our understanding necessarily is limited to the worlds into which we have been born.

III

It should be observed, too, that the process of being "born again" is a two-way affair. It is both revelation and response; it is both being found and it is finding. There is a world of meaning and worth surrounding the newly-born child, a world to which the child responds. Words and gestures from beyond him bid him toward comprehension. Love reaches out with compassionate eagerness, awaiting an answering affection. The flower and the sunset call to his soul with an objective beauty inviting appreciation. History and science compose a body of truth reaching out to embrace the understanding of men. Discovery is our response to something clamoring to be discovered.

"Behold, I stand at the door and knock" [13] is a realistic description of the behavior of the rich variety of values around us. The grace of God is implicit in all rebirth. Knowledge is both gift and achievement; insight is at once a conquest and a contribution; love is revelation plus response; our appreciation of beauty is both finding and being found. Neither knowledge nor love, insight nor appreciation, will "crash the gate" of a closed mind or a shuttered spirit. These gifts of the grace of God await the open door, the prepared spirit; their coming into our lives is contingent on our capacity for response.

The capacity for response, of course, has its stern conditions. Like all birth, it involves an ordeal, for it is a kind of birth. Birth into the physical world demands a union of two cells, nine months of generation and the pain of creation. Birth into the world of science demands the union of discipline and open-minded responsiveness, years of patient study and growing pain as old concepts give way to new. Birth into the realm of art requires a combination of cultivated sensitivity, years of thoughtful observation, and the pangs of disappointment. Just so, birth into the realm of the spirit, wherein we "see God," involves awareness of spiritual need, mourning, meekness, hunger for righteousness, and purity of heart. It is a long road that leads through being something to seeing God.

It is no mystery, this birth into the realm of the spirit wherein we "see God." Obviously, it does not just happen, flashing on us like a meteor from the skies. The bricklayer does not discover the "theory of relativity." It is the scientist, living, moving, and having his being in the realm of science, who perceives new truth. Not the politicians of Rome, but Galileo the scientist discovered the law of the pendulum as he watched the chandelier swinging in the cathedral where he worshiped. Insights come to us in the realms of experience

[13] Revelation 3:20.

wherein we are at home. It is not the artist, not the scientist, not the scholar, but "the pure in heart" who live, in season and out of season, in the realm of righteousness, who achieve the deepest insights into the nature of God. It is not the doctor of philosophy, not the business genius, not the engineer, but the "pure in heart" who "see God." To be sure, the scholar, the business genius, the engineer may "see God," but not by virtue of genius in their specialties. They may well add spiritual "being" to their "doing," and "see God" when they have become the men God intended them to be, achieving a capacity for response to spiritual reality.

Seeing God is an affair of the heart that goes to the very root of our being. What we see is but a reflection of what we are, and what we do not see is a reflection of what we are not. Bernard Lea Rice has it right in his lines:

> I could see God tonight,
> If my heart were right.
> If all the rubbish of my soul
> Were cleared away, my being whole,
> My breast would thrill in glad surprise
> At all the wonder in my eyes.
>
> If my heart were right,
> I could see God tonight!
> And in the radiance of His face
> I'd flame with light and fill this place
> With beauty and the world would know
> The face of God down here below—
> Tonight!
> If only my dull heart were right.[14]

If, with clouded vision and uncertain sight, we "see through a glass darkly," [15] we shall know, if we are wise, that we have missed being "pure in heart."

[14] *Pure In Heart,* by Bernard Lea Rice, Dryden, New York, from *The Christian Century.*
[15] I Corinthians 13:12.

The road to rightness of heart and the vision of God is long and arduous. We do not blunder into Paradise with shrugs and sighs; nor do we muddle through to wholeness and to selfhood in God. "Ye shall seek me and ye shall find me, if ye seek me with all your heart" [16] is no idle word. The road to seeing God leads from an awareness of spiritual need, through honest mourning, to meekness, on through the dusty dryness where we "hunger and thirst after righteousness" and sense our need for the mercy of God. To travel the road demands the total capacity of the total self.

IV

Trying to describe what we mean by seeing God is no easy task. The mystics and the philosophers, the prophets and the seers, all have tried their hand at interpreting for others their own experience of God. They have come away from their labors with a sense of frustration and failure, knowing that words are quite inadequate to reveal what they have seen and known. Trying to describe the experience of God to one who has not shared the experience is like trying to explain football to a Hottentot who never has seen a game. Nevertheless, in our fumbling ways, we go on trying to explain what we never are able to explain fully, to interpret and describe what is forever beyond us. We keep on trying, because, like Peter and John, we must speak of the things we have seen and known and felt, of the things we cannot but share with others, because they have so greatly enriched us.

Seeing God is like looking at the world with eyes of an x-ray machine, which penetrates beneath appearances on the outside to what makes things "tick" inside. There is a quality of inner sight which belongs to the "pure in heart" by means of which they behold God at every turn of the road. They "turn but a clod" and God is there in the creative mystery of

[16] Jeremiah 29:13.

"the good earth." They watch the weaving swallows in their glorious flight, and they exclaim, "This is the finger of God." In the rolling voice of the thunder they hear the voice of His power; beneath the silent stars they find His peace. They see the "flower in the crannied wall" and underneath its fragrant beauty the creative power of God. In the pageantry of the changing seasons, whose glory mocks the garmenture of kings, they see God. They understand the poet's words,

> The poem hangs on the berry bush,
> When comes the poet's eye;
> The street begins to masquerade
> When Shakespeare passes by.[17]

The "pure in heart" see God in what is commonplace to other men.

Some years ago I announced as my sermon title, "God On Main Street," and after the church sexton, a kindly Welshman, had posted it on the bulletin board, he came, with a characteristic twinkle in his eye, to ask, "Ain't He on every street?" He said no more, but it was enough to affirm the deepest insight of "the pure in heart." You and I meet God on our street day after day, but we pass Him by without a nod. Whistler's reply to the attorney who was cross-questioning him during his libel suit against Ruskin is suggestive of the truth. Referring to Whistler's painting *Nocturne in Blue and Silver,* the attorney wanted to know what it represented. Whistler replied, "That depends upon who looks at it." So, what we see on our street depends on who is doing the looking. The "pure in heart" see God on our street and on the Main Streets of the world.

God on our street was as plain to John Calvin as the nose on his face, so that only deliberate blindness could leave anybody unaware of His reality. Anybody afflicted with spiritual

[17] *We See As We Are,* from *"The Thought of God in Hymns and Poems: Second Series,"* by William C. Cannett, The Beacon Press, Boston, 1894, p. 114.

blindness ought to wake up and see what was obvious to the "pure in heart," for God

> ... hath manifested himself in the formation of every part of the world, and daily presents himself to public view, in such a manner, that they cannot open their eyes without being constrained to behold him; ... on all his works he hath inscribed his glory in characters so clear, unequivocal and striking, that the most illiterate and stupid cannot exculpate themselves by the plea of ignorance.[18]

Calvin was overwhelmed by "the infinite splendor" of nature, wherein there was not an atom of the world in which one could not behold some brilliant sparks at least of His glory. God was the Divine Architect of the amazing universe and man. The question really was not worth arguing seriously, because the evidences of God are "everywhere so evident and so obvious, as easily to be distinguished by the eyes and pointed with the fingers." [19]

Wordsworth inherited something of the feeling of Calvin, but he spoke with greater simplicity and gentleness. He opens the inward eye to the reality of the Everlasting in the beauty of the morning hills and in "the grandeur of the forest tree." He is aware of "the Presence"

> Whose dwelling is the light of setting suns,
> And the round ocean and the living air,
> And the blue sky, and in the mind of man:
> A motion and a spirit, that impels
> All thinking beings, all objects of all thought
> And rolls through all.[20]

[18] *Institutes of the Christian Religion,* John Calvin, Westminster Press, Philadelphia, 1936, Vol. I, p. 32.

[19] *Idem.,* p. 64.

[20] *Tintern Abbey,* by William Wordsworth, *The World's Great Religious Poetry,* edited by Caroline Miles Hill, The Macmillan Co., New York, 1944, p. 247.

However, as Elizabeth Barrett Browning thoughtfully suggests, even though "earth's crammed with heaven, and every common bush afire with God," [21] only "they who see take off their shoes." If a man does not see the obvious it is his own fault.

To see God is to be aware of a Reality behind reality and to be sensitive to the pulse of the Everlasting within and around the things we see and feel. It is to find warmth and friendliness behind the majestic sweep of stars. It is to be aware of "a motion and a spirit" that "rolls through all." That awareness is the strength and comfort of "the pure in heart."

V

Beyond awareness is assurance, certainty, profound confidence that God was in Christ, revealing Himself to men. John Baillie insists that "the deepest of all religious experiences is just the act of believing," [22] so that seeing God is simply trusting in the Christ-likeness of God. Seeing God is knowing inwardly that "surely goodness and mercy shall follow me all the days of my life," [23] that He is "refuge and fortress," [24] an ever present help in time of need. There is a suggestion of what that means in the comment of General Protsenko at Stalingrad, when the Russian army there was tottering on the very edge of disaster. Konstantine Simonov has told the dramatic story in his novel, *Days and Nights*. Says the general to one of his captains: "My staff officers had decided to move tonight, but I came back . . . and stopped them. When it's tough the way it is now . . . the soldiers should feel stability. And stability grows in people from feeling that things don't change and partly from feeling that places don't change. So

[21] *Aurora Leigh,* by Elizabeth Barrett Browning, Book VII, line 821.
[22] *The Interpretation of Religion,* John Baillie, Charles Scribner's Sons, New York, 1928, p. 232.
[23] Psalm 23:6.
[24] Psalm 91:2.

long as I can command from here, without moving, I shall command from here." [25] Armies that have not a feeling of dependability and stability of command disintegrate; and lives disintegrate unless they feel a similiar stability of moral and spiritual command.

It is this assurance of the stability and dependability of Christ's command that is the essence of seeing God. "If a man be in Christ he is a new creature," [26] because his life is steadied and guided by a Dependable Command. When the going is tough he does not disintegrate into despair and futility; when the outlook is dark he does not fall apart in pessimistic inertia. He has what it takes to keep going; he breathes hope and confidence into the atmosphere around him. The seductive "Screwtape" who, through the instrumentality of his nephew, one "Wormwood," goes about corrupting Christians in C. S. Lewis' delightful satire, is well aware of the strength of a man's security in God. Therefore, he advises Wormwood,

> The point is to keep a man feeling that he has something other than God, and the courage God supplies to fall back on. So that what was intended to be a total commitment to duty becomes honeycombed all through with little unconscious reservations. [27]

It is the kind of advice you would expect from the devil!

The "pure in heart," plagued by no reservations, find ultimate assurance and peace in their abidingly Dependable Command. "The Lord is my shepherd, I shall not want" [28] is the voice of their confidence, breaking through the doubt of the world. "Jesus Christ, the same yesterday, today and forever" [29] is their word of hope, flung fearlessly on a troubled humanity.

[25] *Days and Nights,* by Konstantine Simonov, Simon & Schuster, New York, p. 125-6.

[26] II Corinthians 5:17.

[27] *The Screwtape Letters,* by C. S. Lewis, Macmillan Co., New York.

[28] Psalm 23:1.

[29] Hebrews 13:8.

He is "the way, the truth and the life" [30] they call to the faltering as they hurl their lives into the future, trusting the wisdom of God's plan of campaign. They are not sentimental, they are sure; they are not troubled, they are triumphant. Like the Crusaders of old, they press on against odds to follow Christ with a shout: "God wills it."

There has been both scholarly and ecclesiastical debate concerning the passage in Matthew wherein Peter is described by the Master as "this rock" on which "I will build my church; and the gates of hell shall not prevail against it." [31] The ecclesiastical structure of the Roman Catholic church is anchored to that passage, and we Protestants have been disturbed by it, when, in reality, it is the charter of our church, too. Not Peter, but Peter's religious experience is the decisive element in the passage: "flesh and blood hath not revealed it unto thee, but my Father which is in heaven!" It was Peter's tremendous insight that was important, his profound spiritual certainty, expressed in the words, "Thou art the Christ, the Son of the living God." [32] The church was built on that experience of God in Christ which yielded the certainty of Dependable Command; it still is being built on the same experience, and the "gates of hell" shall not prevail against it. It is like a mighty tide that cannot be denied. It sweeps over barriers and burrows under walls to undermine the foundations of secular faiths.

The power of our witness and the capacity of the Christian Church to meet the turbulence and truculence of our era depend on our capacity to reproduce in ourselves the experience of St. Peter at Cæsarea Philippi. Our great discovery may come in a very pedestrian way. Most of us do not blunder into bushes like Moses, and God does not strike us down as He struck down Paul on the Damascus Road. More likely, we meet God in some ministry of kindness, and we go away

[30] John 14:6.
[31] Matthew 16:18.
[32] Matthew 16:16.

143

knowing that "inasmuch as ye do it unto one of the least of these" [33] it is done unto Him. Or perhaps, after some lonely vigil beside a loved one who suffers, we come away to say with Jacob, "Surely the Lord is in this place and I knew it not." [34] Perhaps in the patient hours we spend in quiet thought and prayer we may come to understand the words, "Be still, and know that I am God." [35]

It matters not how we come by our experience of God in Christ, whether it steals upon us like "a thief in the night," leaving us warm and glowing inside, or comes by the prosaic way of steady growth in grace and knowledge, so that we never are able to say precisely when we were "born again." The road is not decisive, the destination is; the trail we travel to the heart of Reality is unimportant, but that we get there is vital beyond all imagining. One thing is certain, however, it is the "pure in heart" who know most surely, who find God most certainly, and come away to say, "I know that my redeemer liveth!" [36]

VI

Knowing the dependability of their Command, "the pure in heart" feel the compulsion of a claim. Their escape from uncertainty and inward dividedness requires allegiance to their Saviour. They "see God" in the claim that is laid on them. They "see God" in their inner constraint to action. The fools who sat in the seats of the mighty told Peter and John, two "ignorant and unlearned men" who dared to be "fools for Christ's sake," to cease speaking of their Lord. "We cannot but speak the things we have seen and heard," [37] they answered, and went on testifying to the glory of God in Jesus Christ. They were not just being stubborn and irritat-

---

[33] Matthew 25:40.
[34] Genesis 28:16.
[35] Psalm 46:10.
[36] Job 19:25.
[37] Acts 4:20.

ing; they were under the spell of a Divine compulsion, as was Paul when he cried, "Woe is me if I preach not the gospel." [38] They possessed a splendid secret, and the secret meant life and hope and peace for those who shared it. They felt the compulsion of a splendid claim. How could they be silent?

Have you ever noticed how eagerly we share our pet remedies for what ails us? The other day on a train I said something about my rheumatism to a casual companion. My rheumatism did not amount to much, but it did suggest that the life which begins at forty has some slight irritations. "Ah," said my companion, "I have just the remedy you need." He took out his pen and pad and wrote a list of ingredients and their quantities. "I had rheumatism once," he said, "and I went to an outstanding doctor. That mixture comes straight from him and it will do the trick." I could not help wishing Christians would witness with equal enthusiasm on behalf of the faith that relieves the pain of rheumatic souls. Of course, the man who urged me to try his remedy was enthusiastic about it because it had healed him. The concoction he recommended was "good news"; it was a sort of gospel he had to preach to other sufferers. It had worked for him. His cure imposed a claim; his rescue involved a requirement. He needs must share the secret of his salvation.

To "see God," to find healing and peace in a great assurance, to know the reality of an "inner light" amidst the darkness of the world, is to sense our responsibility for "the healing of the nations." To see God in our own "newness of life" is to be summoned for a task. We have no choice but to say, "Here am I, Lord, send me." [39] Samuel Morrison notes that Columbus, "The Admiral of the Ocean Sea," was "always with God," and that "his frequent communion with forces unseen was a vital element in his achievement." But more, the "conviction that God destined him to be an instrument for spreading the faith was far more potent than the desire to win

[38] I Corinthians 9:16.
[39] Isaiah 6:8.

glory, wealth and worldly honors." [40] Light within for a task without, insight in order to be an instrument of God! Such is the faith of those who see God. Our day desperately needs the pure in heart, who in "seeing God" find healing and light for the task ahead. If it could be said of us,

> The people that sat in darkness
> Saw a great light,
> And to them that sat in the region and
>   shadow of death,
> To them did light spring up,[41]

there would be dignity and a sense of mission in our driving. There would be purpose and power in our living and "the shape of things to come" would offer the promise of the Kingdom.

To "see God" in the knowledge that we have been called for a task, with a Dependable Command to direct us, is to find again the power to do and dare. The secret of our impotence is to be found in the remark John Burroughs once made to Bliss Perry. Mr. Perry proposed that the great naturalist write an essay on a certain topic. "I'd do it," said John Burroughs, "if only I'd get het up enough so's I could flow." But the power to flow, the dynamic of creation, inheres in the discovery that we are called for a task and given stable command for our mission. Moses "endured," pushed on, won the "Promised Land" "as seeing him who is invisible." [42] Seeing God by faith, Abraham discovered a new country. Seeing God, the prophets flung their creative moral challenge to the world.

Being aware of God in the world around us, knowing that "God is in Christ," reconciling the world unto Himself, feeling a claim, a responsibility for His kingdom—these constitute the essence of seeing God. Awareness, assurance, action in the

[40] *Admiral of the Ocean Sea*, Samuel E. Morrison, Little, Brown, & Co., Boston, 1943, p. 47.
[41] Matthew 4:16.
[42] Hebrews 11:27.

Master's name are the trademarks of the pure in heart. Having emerged into the fullness of being in Christ by way of their spiritual pilgrimage they achieve the benediction of final security and power. The "keys of the kingdom" are in their hands. They offer the only promise there is for "the shape of things to come." They alone are prepared to be the peacemakers.

--—❈{ EIGHT }❈—--

PEACE FOR ALL TIME

JUST BEFORE HIS DEATH IN 1940, EDWIN MARKHAM REMARKED
that his fondest hope never had been realized. He had wanted
to write, he said, a poem "which would disperse the armies
of the world."[1] He wanted to expose "the mockery, the futility, the sterility of war" in such fashion that human kind
would turn forever against it. Of course, no one ever will
write such a poem, for peace goes deeper than poetry. We
know without being told that war and human strife are
stupid and we do not need to be persuaded that the mass
destruction of life and of the treasures of the civilized world
is beneath the dignity of the human spirit. It will require
more than poetry to disperse the armies of the world!

The trouble is that it is so much easier to make war than it
is to make peace, to cause strife than to create peace. Anybody
can start a fight, but it takes a saint to stop it. "The war will
last a hundred years, five years of fighting and ninety-five
of winding up the barbed wire,"[2] ran a saying among the
doughboys in 1918. Unfortunately, there were not nearly
enough saints "winding up the barbed wire," and so many
people were scratched and cut that tempers flared and another
war was on in grim earnest. Any would-be Cæsar who gets
scratched can start a war, but peace is more than Cæsars can

[1] Associated Press, April 30, 1939.
[2] *When Johnny Comes Marching Home,* by Dixon Wecter, Houghton
Mifflin Co., New York, 1944, p. 3.

manage. "Blessed are the peacemakers: for they shall be called sons of God." [3]

I

Throughout all the centuries since Jesus lived He has been acclaimed "The Prince of Peace." There are innumerable military leaders who are candidates for the title "The Great," but He alone can wear, without mockery, the name "Prince of Peace." His reign in the hearts of men brings inward "peace that passeth understanding." [4] His reign in the minds of men yields "love, joy and peace" [5] among the sons of men. "Peace I leave with you; my peace I give unto you," [6] He said as He breathed the benediction of His spirit upon His comrades. His business was peace and, as the old hymn has it, "We're here on business for our King." Clearly, then, we were born to be peacemakers after the fashion of our Lord.

Jesus faced the business of making peace among men with a major assumption which is as vital now as it was in His troubled times. He began with the clear perception that we are neighbors under God. He upset the minds of His contemporaries with the blunt assertion that even the Samaritans, whom the Jews hated, were their neighbors. He went so far as to make a Samaritan, of all people, the hero of His unforgettable parable of neighborliness. Paul caught the spirit of his Master when he affirmed that we are "members one of another," [7] and then went on to insist that "there is no Jew nor Greek, but all are one man in Christ." [8] It was strong medicine for a people surrounded by enemies and oppressors; it was too strong to take. Only those who have traveled the road of spiritual pilgrimage through poverty of spirit, mourning, meekness, hunger and thirst after righteous-

[3] Matthew 5:9.
[4] Philippians 4:7.
[5] Galatians 5:22.
[6] John 14:27.
[7] Ephesians 4:25.
[8] Colossians 3:11.

ness, purity of heart, and mercy can take the medicine of peace. It is no easy matter to embrace the Jew and the Negro, to enter the fellowship of classes and creeds other than our own. It is incredibly difficult to batter down the barriers to brotherhood unless we have come to the throne of God to lay our worldly trophies there and to spill our pride on the altar of His love. We cannot begin to be peacemakers until we have achieved union with God, with the source of all power and peace.

The whole world cries out for men and women who will dare to be peacemakers with the light of God in their souls. The world as we know it is eloquent evidence of our failure to face the fact that we are neighbors. The world as we know it is also testimony to the fact that we dwell in a neighborhood. Indeed, the assumption of Jesus had its roots in the cosmos itself, as A. N. Whitehead has shown in his principle of "concretion," wherein everything depends on everything else and the universe is "concreted" in the "flower in the crannied wall" and in the defeat of Napoleon at Waterloo. The truth is strikingly illustrated in the physical universe, where spots turn up, now and then, on the sun, and bits of electricity flash across an abyss of ninety-three million miles to strike the earth's upper, rarefied air. The sky glows with an aurora seen from Hudson Bay to Virginia. A century ago the Northern Lights would have struck the world by their beauty, and men would have gone about their business with nothing but wonder in their hearts. Today it is different. Radio telephones sputter, broadcasting becomes impossible, even cabling is interrupted. A storm on a star stops the complex machinery of a distant planet, and tangled cosmic rays hurl their confusion on a far-away world. The display of the aurora borealis serves to remind us that the solar system is an organism, a structure and not merely a collection of discrete worlds making their rounds year after year. A stupendous event on one world has its repercussions on all the others. We cannot do anything about it, even though our well-organized system of communications is jumbled and snarled beyond calculation. The universe is so nicely balanced, and so integrated that a storm on a star brings panic to a planet. What happens on the distant sun jars on twenty million radio sets and tangles the messages and the news on the airways with which we gird the world.

The auroral display, with its attendant consequences, suggests the interrelatedness of things, and points to the mutual interdependence of the planets and the stars. What is more, it is indicative of the unitary character of the universe, of the fact that we live in a universe, not a multiverse. It tells us something basic about the cosmos in whose orbit we "live and move and have our being," and about the nature of "this sordid place which men call earth." Surely, if the principle of interrelatedness reaches into the cosmos itself as a basic law, it reaches also into human life and we are, as the peacemakers know, bound "in the bundle of life." We are all too well aware that storms within ourselves sweep out beyond the boundaries of our bodies and twist personal relations on Main Street and even in the suburbs of our cities, where our moods are reflected in the behavior of those whose lives are touched by ours! Last night's headache, leaving its day-after hangover, causes indigestion in a whole business organization and throws the lives of more than one out of gear. Yesterday's disappointment, leaving the stamp of bitterness on our today, drips its poison into the family, the school, the office, until what seemed like a personal matter turns out to be a major social concern. Trouble in Tokyo has repercussions in London and Washington; what goes on at Berlin thunders its echoes in Cairo. We are neighbors of all men, as Jesus said we were.

With our cosmos so interrelated, and our lives so bound to the body politic, we are faced with the necessity of making up our minds to be neighborly. When we look into our own lives we shall discover the intimate nature of our relationship not only to those who dwell within the orbit of our glance, but also to those out beyond the scope of our personal reach.

It becomes clear at once that you and I have become what we
are by the give and take of our comradeships and human
contacts. Even Ulysses, who was anything but humble, sensed
how intimately his life was intertwined with those about him.
Speaking for the legendary King of Ithaca, Tennyson says:

> I am become a name
> For always roaming with a hungry heart.
> Much I have seen and known, . . .
> I am a part of all I have met.[9]

He is right, of course, "I am a part of all I have met," but, in
a far deeper sense, all I have met is a part of me. The living
and the dead have conspired to make us what we are. It may
be true, as philosophers contend, that John Locke was only
partly right when he said that the mind is like a blank sheet
of paper on which the impressions of sense are written, but
surely our lives bear the marks of many who came our way,
perchance

> Like ships that pass in the night,
> And speak each other in passing.[10]

Faith and hope and courage are mostly not our own but the
gifts of those with whom we traveled through some tragic
"valley of the shadow." [11] Their wisdom lingers in the insights we have won. Their faith endures within our hearts
like anchors to windward when the storms blow in from the
deep. Their courage lies beneath our surface and seeming as
the often undiscovered "Hero of the Soul."

Henry Adams knew he could not explain himself except as
he traveled back across the years to seek out those who had
shaped his education. He found his memory peopled with a
silent host of men and women whose gentle influence had

[9] *Ulysses,* by Alfred Tennyson, Poetical Works, Houghton, Osgood &
Co., Boston, 1879, p. 56.
[10] *Tales of a Wayside Inn,* by Henry W. Longfellow, Part III, "The
Theologian's Tale," Elizabeth.
[11] Psalm 23:4.

turned his footsteps this way or that. It was not that he was
a robot, moved hither and yon by the wills of other men; it
was rather that he was a sensitive spirit, lighting his candle
and feeding his spirit on the wisdom of those whose insight
was more penetrating than his own. You cannot explain Plato
without Socrates, nor Thoreau without Emerson. You cannot
understand the courage of Timothy building God's kingdom
in a pagan world, except as you see Paul, the man at his back.
You never will fathom the disciples, whose commonplace be-
ginnings promised so little, until you know, as their contemporaries did, that they "had been with Jesus."

Great souls from out the yesterdays of human history have
left their insights on the pages of our many books for us to
light our candles by their knowledge and their wisdom.
Teachers, whose eager minds sought out the best in our heritage of truth, passed on to us the knowledge of the sages of
the earth. Strong men, whose faith was equal to the storms,
preserved the faith we cherish and enriched it for the generations yet to be, their eternal confirmation added to its power.
Poets sensed the pulse of God beating in the silent stars and
swelling through the firmament and left for us the spirit's
rich bequest. Mighty prophets of the truth looked far beyond
this vale of tears and woe to see within the surging turmoil
of the earth the spirit's enduring power to do the will of God.
Our wealth of mind and heart and spirit is not ours but theirs.
Our faith to face the chaos of our days is theirs, and ours only
in so far as we take from their truth what we must to keep an
even keel. To these neighbors, both living and long dead, we
owe a debt too vast to measure.

II

The courage to stand up and take the blows of fate which
beat upon us now depends on the strength we win from our
fellowship with the living and the dead. The pronoun "I"
has an unlovely sound. Its very appearance on the printed

page is unstable, standing there top-heavy, as if a gust of wind might blow it down. But "we" is different; it strikes a solid note; it suggests two leaning on each other, bracing themselves, steadying themselves. "We" can endure what "I" never could face alone; "we" can stand, while "I" surely would go down. It is in the word "we" that we find the symbol of the togetherness of human kind, the comradeship of shared experience and fellowship that makes life worth living and holds the world together in the bonds of peace. Franz Schubert sensed the truth about his own need when he wrote to his friend Schober saying "If only you, Schwind, Kuppel and I were together, then misfortunes would not bother us. As it is, we are separated, each of us in a separate corner. That is my trouble." [12] A wartime survey made in England revealed that among the major causes of crime among youthful offenders fear, worry, loneliness, and homesickness ranked astonishingly high. Commenting on the survey, *Parent-Teacher Magazine* observed, "More than cold and hunger, these youthful criminals felt insecurity, fear, and loneliness. They did not belong to any community, in the sense of being essential."

The truth about ourselves is strikingly suggested in the construction of the Golden Gate Bridge. The central span of 4,200 feet is 700 feet longer than that of the George Washington Bridge. From two graceful cables hangs a sixty-foot roadway flanked by eleven-foot sidewalks. The cables, so delicate to the eye, so strong in reality, are composed of 27,572 wires less than two-tenths of an inch in diameter. Separately, the wires are but threads; banded into rope more than three feet in diameter they support thousands of tons of steel and more thousands of tons of traffic. The strength that lies in union is nowhere more dramatically and powerfully suggested than here. It symbolizes a similar strength and security in human fellowship, a strength able to bear the weight of heavy loads of human woe and hardship. Leaning on each other's strength,

[12] *Franz Schubert, the Man and His Circle,* by Newman Fowler, Tudor Publishing Co., New York, 1935, p. 167.

we are able to sustain the burden of life. We are neighbors in our need and neighbors in our strength.

Like our strength to bear adversity, our wisdom is the product of many minds banded together. Approaching our problem from different directions and bringing to bear on them the varied insights of many backgrounds and differing experiences, we see together what we would not see alone. Like four small boys watching an elephant pass in a circus parade, each of us perceives a different aspect of a single truth. Looking at the elephant in the lead, one boy said, "Wow, look at his trunk"; the second, "Boy, ain't he got big feet?" "Yes," said the third, "his tusks look wicked." The fourth boy added his bit, "Golly, he's big all over." Each lad was impressed by one characteristic of the elephant, and each added a significant dimension to the all-over picture of the animal. Together they saw the elephant. So together we see the truth and achieve a collective understanding of our problems which alone we well might miss. Our knowledge and our wisdom are neighborly achievements!

The faith that many neighbors, seeing partial truth, can meet and reach Truth is basic to the survival of democracy. The faith presupposes, however, as Thomas Jefferson did, that the average man will think for himself and bring his partial truth to the market-place to compete with other half-truths. It assumes that you and I are capable of judgment and that we are tolerant enough to be intellectually honest in our judgments. It operates on the premise that "man is a rational animal" capable of distinguishing between truth and error when they are placed side by side before him. To be sure, these assumptions are on the optimistic side of reality, but they are necessarily the working hypotheses of democratic society. They are valid, too, for the life tenure of untruth is distinctly limited where speech and press are free to trade ideological blows in Times Square. Half-truths are shorn of their deceptive aspects when they face the honesty of a Town Hall, and myths, masquerading as truths, quickly are stripped of their masks in the give and take of public debate. The French Revolutionists were abundantly right in their insistence that freedom is necessary to enlightenment and to the elimination of human error. Surely, in the meeting of many minds truth finds its ultimate triumph, and we achieve a body of truth competent to be the foundation for a worthy peace within the social structure.

Your partial truth and mine, uncorrected by the meeting of many minds, too often lead us "astray in the wilderness," where "we find no city to dwell in." That is why "isolationism" in any form is so dangerous: the "isolationism" of social groups hiding behind walls of self-interest and refusing to meet other social groups on terms of honest tolerance; the "isolationism" of national groups unwilling that their truth should face truth as other nations see it and so discover God's truth; the "isolationism" of political parties erecting opinionated fences around their platforms and refusing to concede the slightest virtue to their adversaries; the "isolationism" of religious bodies retiring "splendidly" behind their stuffy creeds as if they possessed "the truth, the whole truth, and nothing but the truth." Leaders of industry and business dig their own graves with their inflexible opinions when they face the men who toil in their factories and refuse to see any virtue in labor unions. Leaders of labor sow the seeds of the whirlwind which may destroy them when they deal with industrialists as if they were so many robber barons. Nations invite war when they wrap self-righteous robes around their policies and concede no right in other nations. We all need each other and each other's truth if we would build a bridge to bear the cargo of our commonwealth of nations. No peacemaker ever was an isolationist!

Karl Marx, whose implacable hatred of the ruling classes made him blind to their virtues, saw no hope except in violent conflict. He discouraged the meeting of honest minds, opposed tolerance, regretted concessions as preventives of the revolution of which he dreamed. There was none of the peacemaker in his spirit. If he could keep men from seeing eye to eye, and thwart the humanitarianism of his fellow men, upheaval would not be long delayed. Let bitter differences and dangerous extremes emphasize themselves until conflict became inevitable was the essence of his plan for Communist revolution. It suggests the possibility of a reverse process, wherein the meeting of diverse minds and interests begets mutual concessions and builds harmony and social peace. If Karl Marx, who so passionately desired revolution, felt it necessary to discourage mercy and justice and humanitarianism, we who with equal passion desire an ordered social structure have a tremendous stake in cultivating the values he sought to discourage. If he, the revolutionist, hated tolerance, understanding fraternity, and greater economic sharing in the capitalistic world, our devotion to them ought to be a foregone conclusion, creative of peace and amity within our social order.

III

We are, in Walt Whitman's fine phrase, "the clutched together," faced with the necessity of dwelling together in a world neighborhood wherein nations, classes, creeds, and races must live and toil side by side. Minds must meet, revealing stabilizing truths whose validity is acknowledged, else our temporary leaps of progress slide into an ugly depression on the skids of war and strife. I must lean so much on you and you must lean so much on me that both of us are imperiled if we do not understand each other. Walter Lippmann writes, with fine insight, that even

> The thinker, as he sits in his study drawing his plans for the direction of society will do no thinking if his breakfast has not been produced for him by a social process which is beyond his detailed comprehension. He knows that his breakfast depends upon the worker on coffee plantations of Brazil, the citrus groves of Florida, the sugar fields of Cuba, the wheat farms of the Dakotas,

the dairies of New York; that it has been assembled by ships, railroads, and trucks, has been cooked with coal from Pennsylvania in utensils made of aluminum, china, steel and glass. But the intricacy of one breakfast if every process that brought it to the table had deliberately to be planned, would be beyond the understanding of any minds.[13]

Clearly, the fibers which bind us together in "the bundle of life" reach far beyond the intimately personal relationships of everyday experience. We are debtors to every race and tongue, for the fruits of our civilization are the bequests to us of every race and clan. Our anchors are in the philosophy of ancient Greece and in the steady strength of Roman law. Our faith has flowed across the purifying sands of many cultures from the crystal depths of Galilee. Germany gave us Hans Gutenberg and the splendor of the printed page, wherein knowledge of the truth is to be had for the reading. Marconi, a son of sunny Italy, hurled the human voice across the sea on unseen ether waves and opened new horizons for the human mind. Noguchi, whose genius was born in the land of the Rising Sun, turned back the deadly virus of yellow fever and made us masters of a powerful enemy of human life. Louis Pasteur, whose roots went deeply into the soil of his beloved France, shattered ancient superstitions and laid a solid foundation for modern medicine. Sir Isaac Newton, freely thinking on the "tight little isle" that is England, found the secret of our ordered universe and placed the cornerstone for the mighty structure science yet would build. Hugo Grotius, in his simple Danish home, struck out boldly for an order of international law which might become the basis of a lasting peace. All this suggests no nation has possessed an option on the wisdom or the genius of the world; each is debtor to the other in its common life. When our new world is battered into shape it will be seen that it is a product of

[13] *The Good Society,* by Walter Lippmann, Little, Brown & Co., New York, 1937, p. 30.

our joint endeavor and must be held intact by our mutual sufferance.

When we are honest with ourselves and risk strenuous thinking it is clear our lives are so intertwined and we are so dependent on one another that peace and good will are cosmic necessities rather than electives. As Nels Ferré says, "The will to live must become the will to love,"[14] or we cannot live at all. "Love one another"[15] is not simply the naive suggestion of a sentimental soul, but the ultimate condition on which life depends. When love goes out of the relations of men, life goes too, as Horace Walpole suggests so eloquently in his novel, *Blind Man's House,* when he says, "Forsooth, brethren, fellowship is heaven and the loss of it is hell; fellowship is life and the lack of it is death."[16] He goes on, writing with the frenzy of a great conviction which sees the world of our times torn apart by unnatural ideologies and heading into stupid violence, from which we shall be saved only by the power of a compelling idea of human brotherhood. "The idea of Nazi Germany ruling the world has neither bigness nor spiritual grandeur enough," he says, "so it must ultimately fall. Even Napoleon's idea wasn't big enough. A Saint Francis' vision, even a Calvin vision, is big enough creatively, not a Napoleon, and, oh, how much less a Hitler-Goering-Himmler."[17] Love, co-operation, good will—these are the ideas in whose keeping is our only hope. Not conflict but co-operation is the clue to what is truest and deepest in the universe. "And the gates of hell shall not prevail against it."[18]

Quite inescapably, the "Prince of Peace" began with the fundamental assumption that all men are neighbors in a world that demands love and neighborliness as the price of peace.

[14] *The Christian Fellowship,* by Nels E. S. Ferré, Harper & Bros., New York, 1940.
[15] John 13:34.
[16] Doubleday Doran Co., New York, 1941, p. 229.
[17] *Idem.,* p. 229.
[18] Matthew 16:18.

"Blessed are the peacemakers" who feel the reality of neighborhood in God.

IV

Starting with the assumption that all men are neighbors, neighbors in their influence, in their need, in their knowledge and insight and in their courage, Jesus went on to picture in His parable of the Good Samaritan the spirit of neighborliness which begets fellowship and peace. The story has peculiar relevance for our time, because the wounded traveler lying on the road between Jerusalem and Jericho is but a symbol of a wounded, conflict-ridden, bewildered humanity, robbed of its spiritual raiment and stripped of its moral wealth. The ravages of war—moral, material, and spiritual have left mankind bleeding in the ditch, cursing and crying for scapegoats. Wounded men and women are everywhere, lying quite prostrate beside the road. Their mood is one of resentment, bitterness, and mistrust which is on the verge of erupting into conflict and social confusion. Bitterness inevitably breeds bickering and resentment blunders into revolt. Humanity has been infected by wounds that have nothing to do with blood and bandages and by a sickness quite beyond the realm of medicines and drugs. It is the sickness behind the sickness of civilization, the spiritual cancer behind the chaos of the world. It is the greed that ends in grasping, the sin that ends in suffering, the fear that ends in fighting, the ambition that ends in anarchy. Jesus wept over this inward sickness of human kind, a sickness that has poured its poison into the social fabric, turning order into disorder. He knew there could be no peace until the inward ills of men were healed by the brooding love and power of God. Then neighbors could be neighbors.

As Jesus considered the restless, wounded multitudes there was nothing of the monastic about Him, no wish to get away from it all, no priestly passing by "on the other side." Like the Good Samaritan on the road from Jerusalem to Jericho,

Jesus "came where he was." [19] If He retreated to the Mount of the Transfiguration or to the quiet of a garden retreat, it was only that He might return to the market place "in the power of the spirit" to minister more mightily. If He spent the night in prayer it was for the purpose of gaining strength to seek and find the men and women who needed Him, and to breathe on them the benediction of His Peace. When the demoniac raved, the Master "came where he was" to set him free. The "common people heard him gladly" [20] because He sought them out and met their inward needs.

Whenever there was trouble, Jesus was in the middle of it; wherever there was human need, Jesus made His way to it. The sickness of Simon's mother took Him to her bedside, the cry of the centurion sent Him to heal a stricken servant, the moral despair of the woman taken in adultery sent the Master to her side. Wherever a traveler was wounded, Jesus "came where he was," transforming resentment into gratitude. Then quietly He said to his disciples, "As my Father hath sent me, even so send I you." [21] If we listen closely we shall hear Him calling us

> In haunts of wretchedness and need,
> On shadowed thresholds dark with fears.[22]

Those haunts of "wretchedness and need" are everywhere, in palaces as well as in hovels, on Park Avenue as well as in the Bowery. There is a call that comes welling up from the weary multitudes:

> O Master, from the mountain side,
> Make haste to heal these hearts of pain;
> Among these restless throngs abide,
> O tread the city streets again.[23]

[19] Luke 10:33.
[20] Mark 12:37.
[21] John 20:21.
[22] *Where Cross the Crowded Ways,* Frank Mason North, *Presbyterian Hymnal,* Presbyterian Board of Christian Education, Philadelphia, 1945, p. 410.
[23] *Ibid.,* p. 410.

But He cannot "tread the city streets again" unless we tread them for Him. He cannot go where lives are twisted and full of conflict and of nameless pain unless we go for Him. "Feed my sheep," [24] He said to those who followed Him, as if, somehow, they were to be His ambassadors, his "hands and feet" for all the days to come. He would go on living in His disciples, reaching out to wounded travelers with other arms than His own. Through human lips speaking for Him, He would say words of comfort, of courage, and of peace.

The poison that pours into society flows from inward conflict and has its issue in human strife. It is inward turbulence that begets outward confusion. Hurt inside, we strike blindly against society; wounded within, we seek to inflict wounds without. Outward peace cannot be built on inner tumult. "Peace I leave with you. My peace give I unto you," [25] Jesus said, as if, somehow, the inward peace He offered was ultimate, flowing like a living stream into the world. He went about healing wounded minds, cleansing guilty spirits, forgiving tortured consciences. He sought men where they were offering His peace. Now He bids us go for Him.

"He came where he was!" It is bothersome, but there is no way but the patient, plodding way of going where the Master is needed. There is no other way of laying the foundations of social peace save that which seeks the sources of conflict in the inward ills of men. There is no other road to good will among men save that which reaches out to cure the personal infections that so easily end in social disease. If men's hearts are wrong, everything is wrong; if men's minds are wrong, the world is wrong; and the wrongness cannot be cured by aspirin tablets. It can be cured only by an array of peace makers who will "tread the city streets" for the Master, guiding hearts of pain to the only peace there is.

[24] John 21:17.
[25] John 14:27.

V

There is a second sentence that leaps out of the parable of the Good Samaritan to suggest "the mind of Christ," [26] and the spirit of the peace maker. It hangs like a thread at the heart of the narrative and it says, "He saw him." [27] It is a word we need terribly in a generation that has so lost sight of men as men. We see things, and marching around them in terrible array "the vast army of the world's desires." We see ideologies, with men swept en-masse into their emotional maw. We see classes and creeds and colors and national groups, but men elude us, lost in the mass. The man in the multitude has become "the forgotten man" of the world. He is the tool of somebody's idea, the cog for somebody's machinery, the voice for somebody selling something. Our world has turned man into a means without an end!

The man who has lost his significance in the mass is a potent source of conflict, as Richard Wright suggests in his novel, *Native Son*. It is the story of Bigger Thomas, a Negro, struggling blindly for significance, wanting desperately to be somebody in his own right. Living with his family in one room in the "black belt" of Chicago's tenement district, pushed around by the whites, existing on crumbs, he is shriveled by resentment and hate. Day after day, one thought crowds in on his fevered mind: he would be somebody if he dared defy the whites. In his dreams he is forever telling "white folks where to get off." But reality defies his dreams. He is just a cipher, a nobody in a crowded world that engulfed him like the tide. You sense his feeling when, after murder has brought him to the bar of white justice, he says to his lawyer: "Mr. Max, a guy gets tired of being told what he can and what he can't do. You get a little job here and a little job there. You shine shoes, sweep streets, anything. You don't know when

[26] I Corinthians 2:16.
[27] Luke 10:33.

you're going to be fired. You just keep moving all the time, doing what other folks say. You ain't a man no more." [28]

There you have life's ultimate tragedy: "You ain't a man no more." Insignificant, unwanted, unneeded, lost in a tide of color—that is deadly. No wonder men protest against it, even as Bigger did, with crime and violence. Nobody wants to be nobody, and today the "nobodies" are on the march, intent on being somebodies. Their hearts are set against the some-bodies who stand in their way. It is in such conditions that Communism, with its class hatred, finds fertile ground. The tragedy is at the heart of the social struggle we see on every hand.

But as for Jesus, "He saw him," the little man like Bigger Thomas, lost and hurt in the crush of the mass, as somebody in his own right. He saw him as a child of God, with hopes and dreams and possibilities worth drawing to the surface. The "ninety and nine" might be safe and sound; but God was "ever mindful" of the Prodigal.

Some time ago in Chicago I was standing in the Santa Fe Station waiting for my train when a West Coast train pulled into the station. The jam of waiting people was almost beyond belief, and all eyes were on the trainshed where a contingent of soldiers was unloading. I was standing beside a man and woman whose boy was on that train. They were standing on tip-toe, utterly unaware of the mob, unmindful of the press of people. They saw their boy, then, and tears brimmed over in the woman's eyes and slid down her cheek. "I'm being silly," she said to her husband as she wiped away her tears. Her husband gulped and his Adam's apple jumped up and down as if it could not find a comfortable place to stop. "Me, too," he answered, and blew his nose vigorously. Then the lad, a young captain, was in his mother's arms and then pump-ing his father's arm. His uniform was covered with ribbons, battle stars, the purple heart and oak leaf clusters. So far as

[28] *Native Son,* by Richard Wright, Harper & Bros., New York, 1940, p. 299.

his mother and father were concerned, he was the one man in the multitude; it was not the crowd, but one boy in it that mattered. They "saw him."

Jesus was like that mother and father in the station waiting for their boy to come home, except that the boys coming home were all His boys. "Who are my father and mother, my brothers and sisters?" He asked, as if to say that He saw them there in the crowd—the baffled and confused, the hurt and the troubled. He was standing tip-toe, seeing them in the multitudes, flashing a smile of welcome, offering a hand in greeting, throwing his arms around those who would answer his smile. The multitudes were significant because of the individual men in the crowd; congregations in the market-place or beside the Sea of Galilee were not just conglomerations of men in the mass, they were Mary and Joseph, James and Peter, Stephen and Barnabas. Jesus saw them one by one and though he spoke to them multitudes at a time, he really spoke to each one. There was the tired woman, weary with toil, trying to guide her children aright: "He saw her." There was the lad, wrestling with temptation and really wanting to be himself: "He saw him." There was the lonely man, wrestling with a sick body and trying to keep on going for the sake of his children: "He saw him." No wonder Jesus was "the Prince of Peace."

VI

He had to see men one by one, of course, before He could take the next step with the Good Samaritan: "He had compassion on him." [29] Compassion is what you feel when your small child catches his finger in the door of the automobile. It hurts you as much as it hurts him! It is what you feel when your daughter is disappointed or terribly hurt about something. You suffer as much as she suffers. You would do anything under heaven to make it different, endure any sacrifice

[29] Luke 10:33.

to make her way easier. You enter into her suffering, share
it and suffer as she suffers. You cannot eat and you cannot
sleep for her sake.

There is a strange sentence which describes the feeling of
Moses about his people before his burning bush experience.
It says that he saw his people and "looked on their burdens." [30]
Jesus felt the burdens of His people, they were His burdens;
their hurts were His hurts; their frustrations were His frustrations. He had "compassion" upon the Rich Young Ruler who
came seeking the secret of eternal life and "loved him." [31]
He felt the struggle within the young man turned sadly away
from the harsh terms of life that is life. He felt the shame of
the woman taken in adultery and the perplexity of Nicodemus. He never gazed down upon life from the balcony;
He entered into and deeply shared the experiences of those
whose lives He touched.

There is a touch of emotion in compassion, and we must not
be afraid of it. The problems of others cannot be dealt with
at arms' length. We cannot hold them off like a scientist ob-
serving reactions with detachment and pure objectivity. Years
ago I used to go to a dentist who was a master of the art of
repairing faulty teeth. When he fixed a tooth it stayed fixed
and I am grateful for that. But he was entirely ruthless about
my feelings. He never padded my pain with a word that
suggested he knew how it felt. So far as he was concerned,
I was supposed to know there is no such thing as painless den-
tistry, and if I did not know it, that was my misfortune. When
he went to work on a decayed tooth, there was no compassion
in him. He would have been a better dentist and certainly
more popular if he could have mixed his skill with a bit of
compassion. Even a drill biting into a tooth hurts less if the
dentist appears to be aware of the hurt and at least a little
sorry about it. I'll grant that a compassionate spirit would
take something out of the dentist. It would cost something

[30] Exodus 2:11.
[31] Mark 10:21.

in terms of emotional strain, but it would be helpful to his patients.

Compassion is not pity that looks down; it is love that shares and divides the poignancy of pain. It does not condemn the failures and the feeble, the sinner nor the fool. It tries to understand. It takes for granted the fact of human sin and the universal need of all men for the redeeming grace of God. The compassionate take seriously the gentle caution of the Master about seeing the splinter in a neighbor's eye while missing the timber in their own. They sense the truth inherent in Abraham Lincoln's story of an old man who lived on the bank of the Wabash River. One day the old man thought he saw a squirrel in a nearby tree. He got his rifle and fired; but the squirrel still sat in the tree; he fired again and again. His son, wondering what the shooting was about, came running. "Do you see that squirrel about half-way up yonder tree?" the old man asked. "Naw," replied the lad. Then looking closely at the old man, he said, "I see your squirrel, you've been shooting at a louse on your eyebrow." [32] The tragedy of much of life inheres in the unhappy fact that we spend all too much time shooting at the sins of our neighbors without realizing that we are shooting at a louse on our own eyebrow. The compassionate man, the peace-maker, starts with his own sin, sensing his need for righteousness and purity of heart.

One of the strangest of all the sayings of Jesus shames our human pride and self-righteousness. There came one saying, "Good Master," and before the words were out, Jesus answered, "Why callest thou me good? There is none good but the Father." [33] With the insight of the Everlasting, the Prince of all peace-makers set the stage for His peacemaking with a Divine affirmation of His humility before the Father. You see, there is no such thing as a proud peace-maker; that is a con-

[32] *Abraham Lincoln,* Vol. I, by Carl Sandburg, Charles Scribner's Sons, New York, 1926, p. 357.
[33] Matthew 19:17.

tradiction in terms. There can be no peace until we see we all have sinned, until we say with humble pain, "It's me, O Lord, it's me, standin' in the need of prayer." Unfortunately, we have a devastating habit of forgetting that human nature is human nature from Tokyo to London and from Berlin to Washington. The sins of men and nations are strangely alike and the things we despise in others, others see in us. Our sins may be different in degree, but they are the same in essence. Waldo Frank suggested the painful truth before the war began when he came home from traveling in the Axis countries and asked the question, "What if what made them is in us?" Surely no one can view the American scene today without being frightfully troubled by that penetrating question.

In the final days of the Civil War, Abraham Lincoln dared to say that the war between the states was the bitter fruit of the sins of both the North and the South. Such was the conviction of a peace-maker who could then go on to say that the peace must be built on compassion, "with malice toward none and charity for all." The major tragedy of American history, a tragedy whose consequences still endure, is that those who finally made the peace between the states were proud and arrogant in their self-righteousness with no compassion in them. They forgot they, too, had sinned. I am haunted by that devastating parable of Jesus, spoken

"unto certain who trusted in themselves that they were righteous, and set all others at naught. Two men went up to the temple to pray; the one a Pharisee and the other a publican. The Pharisee stood and prayed thus with himself. God, I thank Thee that I am not as the rest of men, extortioners, unjust, adulterers, or even as this publican. I fast twice in the week; I give tithes of all that I get. But the publican, standing afar off, would not lift up so much as his eyes unto heaven, but smote upon his breast saying: God be merciful unto me, a sinner. I say unto you, this man went down to his house justified, rather than the other; for everyone that exalteth

himself shall be humbled, but he that humbleth himself
shall be exalted." [34]

That parable speaks with warning urgency to us, for there can
be no peace save that which is born of a humility and compassion rooted in the consciousness of our common sin.

The Chinese have a saying that is pertinent to our human
predicament: "To keep afloat in a leaky boat, both must
bail." [35] In our homes when conflicts rage, the boat will sink
unless both parties to the conflict bail out their faults. In our
business relationships when there is friction, not one, but all
must bail out their sins in common recognition of their mutual
wrong. When industry and labor rage against each other
amidst strife and strikes, no peace can come until they both
begin to bail, casting out the greed that is their common sin.
"The best of men are as briars, the most upright a prickly
hedge," is the prophet's way of saying we all have much to
bail.

The peace-maker, having traveled the road through spiritual
need, to mourning, to meekness; through passion for righteousness, to purity of heart well knows the power of evil and
the deceptive ways of human motive. Well does he know his
own wrestling with "principalities and powers" [36] is not done;
that only incessant bailing makes him worthy as a child of
God. He sees himself with honest eyes, sensitive to the seductive ways of wrong, and he is humble and compassionate.
There is no room for pride, for hard unyielding self-righteousness, in his soul. His peace-making has its roots in compassion.

The significance of compassion lies in the fact that, instead
of repelling, it draws men unto itself. It cares so much for
others that others care deeply in response. It invites confidences and unlocks the secretive tongue; it draws out the
festering secret, the gnawing sin: it breaks down the stout

[34] Luke 18:9-14.
[35] *Shake Hands With the Dragon,* by Carl Glick, Whittlesey House,
1941.
[36] Ephesians 6:12.

barriers that the self erects to preserve its pride. It inspires the humility which is back of any redeeming repentance. So as Jesus walked about, men sought Him out and heard Him through and ended by leaning their lives upon His Father. In His compassion, men found their chance and will to begin life over again. The failures like Zaccheus, were nerved to make moral restitution for their wrongs. The publicans with whom He ate to scandalize the good, found their will to righteousness renewed. There were times when the Master's prescription for new life bit and hurt like the dentist's drill, but the hurt was healed by the compassion behind it. Indeed, there is redeeming power in the word, "He had compassion on him." Where there is compassion, there is peace.

VII

There is a final word, too, which is the fruition of all the others: "He bound up his wounds." [37] It was but natural for the compassionate spirit who cared for men one by one to bind up the wounds of the hurt. It was not merely a matter of bandages and oil, either, for he who heals the body heals but half the ills of men. What Jesus offered was a kind of perpetually working penicillin to eliminate moral gangrene and spiritual pneumonia. He offered God, the Great Physician, whose healing touch deals like magic with the worst of men's wounds and hurts. He understood that our human devices for dealing with hurt minds and baffled spirits are only make-shifts, poor substitutes for "the power of the spirit" [38] to make men truly whole. He bound up the wounds of men with God!

And what a God! He is no mysterious deity hidden behind the mists of the Milky Way, but one "nearer than hands and feet." He holds out His open arms to the Prodigal Son, returning after wasting his substance in riotous living. Like a

[37] Luke 10:34.
[38] Luke 4:14.

Good Shepherd He pushes out into the storm of the world's turbulence to find the lost and reclaim the bewildered. He knows the sparrows in their flight and the lilies that fling their fragrance upon the meadow. The heavens declare His glory and the firmament showeth His handiwork, and underneath are His everlasting arms gentle with compassion. He calls the little children unto Him, forbidding them not, for they are His. "I am the Lord which exercise loving kindness . . . in the earth." [39]

Jesus said He was what He was and did what He did because God was what He was and did what He did. "I and the Father are one," [40] He said as He "went about doing good." [41] It was not He, it was God. It was not Jesus who forgave the paralytic and gave him strength with which to bear the bed upon which he had suffered, it was God in Him. It was not Jesus who healed the sick and caused the blind to see; it was God. "Why calleth thou me good? There is none good but the Father" [42] was His way of pointing to the power behind Him and showing the source of His goodness and strength. He was not trying to do a patchwork job of healing and helping with bandages and court-plaster; He wanted to get down to the bone of the matter—to God. He wanted men to know that He, Jesus, was not on His own. He was an instrument of God. Indeed, He was so effectively God's instrument that men said, "God was in Christ, reconciling the world unto Himself," [43] and men to each other.

It is as instruments of God, revealing His love in ourselves, pointing to a power not ourselves making for righteousness, mercy and forgiveness, that we bind up the wounds of men with peace and good will. It is by way of our own spiritual pilgrimage, leading from poverty of spirit to the vision of God

[39] Jeremiah 9:24.
[40] John 10:30.
[41] Acts 10:38.
[42] Mark 10:18.
[43] II Corinthians 5:19.

that we become worthy instruments of peace and good will among men, binding up the wounds of bitterness and hatred with the love of the Father. And seeing the wounded and the sick in the multitude, the sources of infection within the body of society, Jesus "came where he was. He saw him. He had compassion on him. He bound up his wounds." He did not stop there, however. He went on to say: "Go thou and do likewise." [44] Such is the charter of those of whom the Master said: "Blessed are the peacemakers, for they shall be called the children of God."

To be sure, the peace-makers pay a price for their peace-making. The moral principles undergirding orderly society demand heroic spirits, prepared, as Jesus said, to risk persecution if need be for the sake of their creed. So we turn to the risk—and the reward.

[44] Luke 10:37.

NINE

RISK IN PASSING THROUGH

A CHILDHOOD STORY, PUSHING ITS WAY INTO MY MEMORY, SUG-
gests there are perils in passing through the gates to greatness.
A striking picture illustrated the story. In the picture an
armor-clad knight sat on a pure white horse before a massive
iron gate, slowly swinging open on its rusty hinges. The
knight, so the story ran, had spent months seeking the City
of Gold. As he spurred through the gate his eyes rested on the
fabulous city he had sought so long. Its jeweled spires glis-
tened in the distance. Sitting his horse a moment before riding
on toward the city, he was startled by a fairy whispering in
his ear, "A dragon lies in wait betwixt thee and the fair city.
Many," she said, "have come thus far, but none has passed the
dragon's lair. Beware! Only the brave ride on." Undismayed,
the knight rode on to conquer the dragon and inherit the
City of Gold.

The story is a parable of human experience. We journey
through the gates to greatness, seeking to fulfill in our lives
the implications of the Beatitudes of Jesus, and then we
blunder into dragons. Indeed, the Master was aware of the
risk in passing through the gates. "Behold," He says, "I send
you forth as sheep in the midst of wolves," [1] as if being religious meant inviting the wolves to do their worst. "Then
shall they deliver you up into tribulation, and shall kill you;
and ye shall be hated of all nations for my name's sake." [2]

[1] Matthew 10:16.
[2] Matthew 24:9.

Here is no promise of security and comfort as the reward for righteousness. Instead, "they shall put you out of the synagogues," [3] and persecute you. Nevertheless, "Blessed are they that have been persecuted for righteousness' sake: for theirs is the kingdom of heaven." [4] It is a strange religion that promises not comfort, but a cross; not security, but suffering; not triumph, but tribulation. As Jesus saw the matter, religion belonged on a cross more often than it belonged on cushions. It was a daring point of view; it left the Pharisees in a state of indignant protest. Why should anybody want to be religious if the reward was to be a cross instead of a crown? Why should anyone wish to pass through the gates to moral and spiritual greatness only to meet dragons?

I

Jesus, however, was a realist before He was anything else. He knew Main Street well enough to be keenly aware of the skullduggery that went on there, and He had seen enough of life in the synagogue to know the meaning of intolerance and prejudice. The world was not growing better and better of its own accord; it would have to be made better by way of "peril, toil and pain." Mark Twain took a long look at humanity with his sensitive, humorous eyes and came to the conclusion that men were so bad they really were not worth saving. He said that when he got to heaven, if that good fortune should fall to his lot, he was going to suggest that God instigate a new flood. He wanted no Noahs left behind, however, to start the human race again.

Plunged into bankruptcy through the dishonesty of another, Mark Twain made the common mistake of assuming that the righteous ought to get along swimmingly. Jesus, on the other hand, began His career on the assumption that the righteous were "trouble-born stars." His life was motivated by the con-

[3] John 16:2.
[4] Matthew 5:10.

viction that the righteous belonged wherever there was wrong needing to be made right, wherever there was sin needing salvation, wherever there was chaos needing to be transformed into order. "I am come," He said earnestly, "to send not peace but the sword," [5] as if whoever dared to follow Him must face unending struggle. The righteous, as Jesus saw it, are God's "trouble shooters."

Jeremiah the prophet, who endured the scorn of his country-men for the sake of the truth, had no wish to be a "trouble shooter." "Oh that I had in the wilderness a lodging place of wayfaring men," he wrote, "that I might leave my people and go from them! for they are all adulterers, an assembly of treacherous men." [6] He felt somewhat the way we feel when we sing, "I'll build a sweet little nest somewhere out in the West and let the rest of the world go by." There is an urge in all of us "to get away from it all." But Jeremiah, like Jesus, sensed that the righteous had no business burying themselves in monasteries to avoid the onerous necessity of dealing creatively with the wrongs of the world. None spoke more powerfully than he against the sins of his people. That was his business as a righteous servant of God.

Unhappily, a large portion of the righteous in our time have been haunted by the monastic mood. In politics, the righteous have been reluctant to soil their hands. "I'd like to do some-thing," we say, "but I'm not going to get out on a limb." We know all too well that we had better stand against the tide of anti-Semitism in our time, but we want no arguments about the question. Let the Jews take care of themselves, we say, washing our hands of the problem. We know instinctively that our treatment of the Negro in our midst is unworthy of our professed Christianity, but it is safer to ignore the issue than to face it with grim honesty. Our monastic mood will yet be our doom. The truth is that we Christians belong in the middle of explosive situations, wherever they are. If there

[5] Matthew 10:34.
[6] Jeremiah 9:2.

is a squabble in our club, it is not Christian to send a letter
of resignation. If the office force is divided, and feud has
flared, we belong in the middle of the feud, standing steadily
for what is right. If the family has come almost to the point
of blows, being righteous does not mean packing bags and
leaving for points remote. If somebody is about to put over a
dishonest deal, being righteous does not mean turning away
and resolving to "see no evil, hear no evil, and think no evil."
If things untrue and downright false are being said, silence
is not the reaction of the righteous.

There is a familiar story of the fisherman, angling at the
base of a drawbridge, opened for a passing boat, and watching
a blind man blunder toward the bridge. "By gum," he said
to himself, "if somebody doesn't stop that blind man he'll fall
in." He went on with his fishing, spat vigorously. "By gum,
he'll fall in sure," he repeated. There was a scream and a
splash. Then, with a shrug of the shoulders, the fisherman
remarked, "By gum, he has fallen in." The story is a terrible
parable of our human behavior. As John MacKay says regret-
fully, we have a "balcony" way of living remote from the vital
issues of our time. We watch while men flounder toward
disaster, we look on unmoved while evil has its way with men,
we sit as mere spectators while the world blunders toward war
and chaos. Certainly, there is no danger watching from a
balcony while conflict rages in the street below. There is no
risk in being neutral, and when the evil wins the fray we can
say we had no part in its triumph. We are not to blame.
Nevertheless, the Scriptures suggest God's disgust with those
who are neither hot nor cold. "I will spew them out of my
mouth," [7] saith the Lord. It is the cowardice of silent indifference to the perpetual crisis in the affairs of men that is the
sin of so many. "He that is not with me is against me" [8] was
Jesus' way of pushing the neutral fence sitters from their pre-

[7] Revelation 3:16.
[8] Matthew 12:30.

carious perch. "Take up thy cross and follow me" [9] where rough waters run and the rapids foam. "Follow me" where goodness is dangerous and righteousness is costly, or be against Me and Mine. How can anyone look on Jesus and see Him baffled, crowned with thorns, spat upon and nailed to a cross, without seeing what righteousness meant to Him? "He set his face steadfastly to go to Jerusalem," [10] marched into trouble with His eyes open, challenged wrong within the temple gates and invited evil to do its worst. There was nothing monastic about the mind of Christ; He lived and died trying to make things right on Main Street.

II

Quite inevitably, righteousness that is worth anything demands a willingness to be hurt. A man cannot stand for the right against the wrong without being bruised now and then. A football referee once was asked about a certain player in a game he had refereed. "I can say only this," he answered, "I never have had to pull him out from the bottom of a scrimmage. I often have found him on top of a pile of players, where he had jumped after the man with the ball had been stopped by another player. He never was the first to make the tackle." [11] The world is full of people like that, and it is a safe game to play. Nobody ever gets hurt if he waits until the ball is down before making his tackle, and, of course, he is not much use to his team, either.

No man is really righteous until he is willing to be hurt if need be for his righteousness, like Woodrow Wilson, broken in body and mind for the sake of a dream that was new; like William Wilberforce, willing to endure hate and animosity in England to set the black man free. Righteousness is doing

---

[9] Matthew 16:24.
[10] Luke 9:51.
[11] *The Acts of the Apostles,* Vol. II, by Halford Luccock, Willett, Clark & Co., 1939, p. 150.

what is costly for the sake of what is right. It is speaking the truth at the expense of votes, as did Abraham Lincoln. It is sacrificing a business contract on the altar of a moral conviction, as many an honest business man has done. It is rejecting an unreasonable lawsuit and losing the fee for the sake of an ideal of justice, as many a lawyer has done.

The spirit of righteous risk for Christ's sake is revealed in the behavior of a brilliant young Englishman, a lord. He had political ambitions and great gifts of mind and heart, but he came to see the poverty, squalor and despair that weighed so heavily on the poor of London. The time for decision had come, and Lord Shaftesbury was faced with a difficult choice. Which should it be, politics or the poor? Through a long night Shaftesbury struggled with temptation akin to that of Jesus in the wilderness. One by one, he uprooted his own desires, calling, "Here am I, Lord, send me" to fight the battles of the poor. There was in London a guild of thieves, and no one but a thief, proven to the satisfaction of the members, could be a member. Even these dregs of society turned to Shaftesbury as friend and guide. He flung his life against the evil of child labor, and for his trouble he was persecuted and hated by men in power. They called him a "radical," and no doubt they would have called him a "red," if the Communists had amounted to much in his time. When Shaftesbury died, all England turned out to honor his name. Strange and yet glorious were the banners that followed him to the grave: "I was a stranger and ye took me in." [12] "I was in prison and ye visited me." [13] "I was hungry and ye gave me to eat." [14] Here, indeed, was righteous risk inheriting the kingdom.

The world has a subtle, treacherous way of dealing with men who dare to be too righteous. Like little boys calling names across the back fence, men call the disturbers of their unfettered greed by such names as "Communist," "Socialist,"

[12] Matthew 25:35.
[13] Matthew 25:36.
[14] Matthew 25:35.

"Red," as if, somehow, the names nullified the disturbing voice. Tag a man with a label like "radical" and respectable people are horrified. Many a man, intent on defending justice, has found his righteousness short-circuited by a label he could not shake. Evil is a past master in the use of the red herring! But the peril of a discrediting label is part of the risk of righteousness. Men called Jesus "blasphemer," "seditionist," emissary of Beelzebub, "sinner," and did their best to destroy His influence. He took it in His stride, remembering that the prophets had been persecuted before Him.

Beware when all men speak well of you! It may be healthy from a business point of view, but it is not healthy spiritually. All men spoke well of the self-deceived prophets who always made "the worse appear the better part" for the kings they served with slavish cowardice. Diogenes, hunting in midday with a lighted lantern for an honest man, would be harder put to find a prophet among the popular "men about town." Prophets are not popular. Nobody loves a gadfly like Socrates, puncturing the pretensions men cherish and proving the absurdity of their stupid opinions. Anybody can be popular if he can be eloquent in saying what everybody believes, serving merely as a sounding board for our social convictions. Nevertheless, from an historical point of view, "everybody" frequently has been wrong, and only the prophetic remnant right. Genuine righteousness is likely to be lonesome, and rather on the unpopular side. Socrates was right, but he stood almost alone; Jeremiah was right, but strictly on the lonesome side; Jesus was right, but even His disciples "left him and fled." [15]

When a man is willing to be hurt or labeled or lonesome for the sake of righteousness, he is made of the stuff of the prophets, and he has some chance of making a creative contribution to the world. Somebody has to ride off on a tangent from society to blaze new trails to better, nobler days. As someone has noted, "a policy of drift gathers only barnacles." Mud-

[15] Matthew 14:50.

dling through without moral direction is altogether normal, but quite stupid. A man can join the muddlers with no invitation fee, but prophetic righteousness comes high: it is costly but it is creative. Just as the telegraph followed the trail of the Pony express, so, in the end, humanity follows the trails blazed by its prophets of righteousness who are willing to risk the dangers of new trails. Voltaire went off on a wide tangent from the French monarchy with his plea for "liberty, fraternity and equality," but he was on a moral trail, and France slowly got around to his way of thinking. John Milton, disturbed by his country's policy of moral and political drift, cut loose from the social moorings of his time, and helped to lay the foundations for a new freedom in England. He understood, however, that

> Long is the way and hard,
> That out of hell leads up to light.[16]

Humanity usually has persecuted its prophets, preferring to remain in hell rather than climb to the light. Nevertheless, there is no stopping a moral idea whose time has come. "Blessed are they that have been persecuted for righteousness' sake: for theirs is the kingdom of heaven," and theirs is the earth as well, but they do not live long enough.

There is a glorious paragraph in Katherine Butler Hathaway's *The Little Locksmith,* which, somehow, condenses the spirit of risk which is a corollary of righteousness. She says:

> O lucky beyond most human beings is the . . . person who comes upon an utterly unfamiliar island flat in the middle of his fate-line, and who is bold enough and crazy enough to defy the almost overwhelming chorus of complacency and inertia and other people's ideas and to follow the single, fresh, living voice of his own destiny, which at the crucial moment speaks aloud to him and tells him to come on.[17]

[16] *Paradise Lost,* by John Milton, Book II, Line 432.
[17] Coward-McCann, Inc., New York, 1942, p. 3.

There is that "come on" quality about all our moral visions, and blessed is he who dares "to follow the . . . living voice of his own destiny" to righteousness and peace in God.

III

The prophets and the spiritual pioneers who have dared to be "persecuted for righteousness' sake" have first traveled the road of spiritual pilgrimage from awareness of spiritual need to the power of a splendid faith in the righteous will of God. They have not stood alone against the dragons beyond the gates. They have stood with God, certain that He is Lord of history. In meekness they have sat down humbly before the facts of human experience to understand, as John Calvin did, that the convulsions of history are the consequences of the moral failure of men. Only "vigorous opposition" to "immense evils" could redeem history. "Without the shedding of blood there is no remission," [18] is an eloquent statement of the costliness of that "vigorous opposition."

The plight of our times suggests that "vigorous opposition" to evil has been too costly for our frail faith to bear. We have asked petulantly with Edwin Arlington Robinson:

> What does it mean, this barren age of ours?
> Here are the men, the women and the flowers,
> The seasons and the sunset as before,
> What does it mean? [19]

The answer is all too clear. We have blundered into a barren age because there have been too few men and women daring to be "persecuted for righteousness' sake." We have enshrined ourselves, our gold, our nation and left God to pick daisies. His righteous will, however, is smashing the half-gods we have worshiped. That is the meaning of our barren age. Our

[18] Hebrews 9:22.
[19] "Sonnet," Edwin Arlington Robinson, *Collected Poems,* The Macmillan Co., New York, 1937, p. 93.

ears, deafened by the roar of the wide world, no longer hear the voice of the prophet crying, "Cease to do evil; learn to do well." [20] It is not until we have climbed the steep ascent from awareness of spiritual need to vibrant faith in the righteous will of God that we dare to risk righteousness with assurance of final triumph. If the "judgments of God are true and righteous altogether" we make no mistake in gambling our lives on righteousness. Amos, the vine dresser of Tekoa, took his stand against the evils of his time, and risked his life for righteousness, knowing he stood on solid ground. He predicted the fall of Israel at a time when Israel was prosperous and strong, but morally dissolute. And Israel fell. Without scientific historical knowledge to guide them, led only by their faith in the moral trustworthiness of reality, the prophets looked at the greatest empires the world had seen, the Assyrian and the Babylonian, and measuring them by the canons of right and wrong, pronounced their doom. From the materialistic point of view, the prophets had everything against them, and everything was against them except the moral fibers of God's universe. "Surely the wrath of man shall praise thee!" [21]

The prophets would be amused by our "economic interpretation of history" and our frantic efforts to save ourselves by tinkering with our systems. They would see that systems have their little day and perish for lack of undergirding moral dispositions in the hearts of men and women. Not systems, but men are at fault, they would say; not economic orders, but moral attitudes. It is the fact, as Thomas Moore said, that "men like ravenous fishes would feed on one another" that wrecks the systems we build. Shakespeare said much the same thing in King Lear through Albany, who observes to Goneril:

> If that the heavens do not their visible spirits
> Send quickly down to tame these vile offenses
> It will come.

[20] Isaiah 1:16-17.
[21] Psalm 76:10.

Humanity must perforce prey on itself
Like monsters of the deep.

All this suggests the realism of a moral interpretation of history which reads our chaos and our woe in terms of lack of moral discipline. We have cracked up against the moral will of God which rules our little days. "God the Father Almighty" is Lord of history even though He be, like Israel, "despised and rejected of men." [22] Knowing that, the righteous dare to be persecuted for His sake.

IV

The righteous, who risk persecution, know also that God is Lord of the self. There is in all of us a "divine discontent," which is pacified only by our persistence in righteousness, regardless of the cost. No matter what life's hard realities do to us, our moral aspirations still claim authority over us. No matter to what depths of sin we may descend, we are constrained by moral demands that will not let us go. We may disregard the mandates of the will of God that haunt us, but we cannot avoid feeling their reality. We may seek escape from them by subtle sophistries which attempt to make "the worse appear the better part," but for all the ruses we employ we are burdened by unquenchable remorse. We may deny the right of these unreasoned, unwanted mandates to determine the way of our going, but when we have defied them they mock our misery with a defiant, "I told you so." "If I ascend into heaven, thou art there; if I make my bed in hell, thou art there," [23] is the Psalmist's way of saying that the demands of God reach from the heights to the depths of the universe. If we run from them, they pursue us relentlessly, like Francis Thompson's "Hound of Heaven"; if we rest, they plague our fitful slumber. When, in the midst of our absorption in other things, we think we have securely locked the doors against

[22] Isaiah 53:3.
[23] Psalm 139:8.

them, a key turns lightly in the lock and there they stand as if to say, "We are a part of yourself. You cannot lock us out."

Philosophers and poets and saints have been saying through the ages it is no "dreaming, dark, dumb thing" that rules our lives, and that the world is no "tale told by an idiot," "signifying nothing," [24] if we are perpetually haunted by the challenge to assume the risks of righteousness despite our wishes and desires. It is not the voice of our own egos that commands our respect for the truth, for the voice defies our own wishes and what seems to be our safety. It is not merely the strength of social custom that binds us to the higher good, for the good we know we needs must do is nobler than the ethic of the herd. We are condemned, not by the tolerant standards of a crowd, for we are good enough to "get by" in ordinary society where sin is a cherished luxury, enjoyed by the "best people"; but we are not good enough to satisfy the imperatives we feel within. Men sense a Spirit that is seeking them, a Voice that is calling, a Presence that has "beset them behind and before and laid its hand upon them." No matter where we turn

> Still with unhurrying chase
> And unperturbed pace,
> Deliberate speed, majestic instancy,
> Came on the following Feet,
> And a Voice above their beat.[25]

These facts of your experience and mine lead the humble-minded to an unfailing faith that the values and ideals which live in our highest aspirations have their anchors in a universe that cares deeply for them. They will neither die nor cease from pursuing us, because they have their being in the Great Goodness at the heart of things as they are. They are not dependent on our fickle ways, for their reality is in the moral will of God. Defeat will not destroy them; disaster will not

[24] *Macbeth*, by William Shakespeare.
[25] *The Hound of Heaven*, by Francis Thompson, *Contemporary Poetry*, edited by Marguerite Wilkinson, The Macmillan Co., 1933, p. 237.

overwhelm them; indifference will not crush them. Yes, though, like Viviano, we announce proudly, "We have extinguished the heavenly lights in a magnificent gesture," they will go on burning in spite of us.

It is because God lives in men as moral will that we find satisfaction only when we answer the mandates of "the heavenly lights." "This is the life," we say in the midst of our revelry, but the wine which we thought was the "Wine of Good Hope" turns out to have been pressed from the "Grapes of Wrath." When our night of folly is done and we have claimed to the full the gifts of sordid life, we cannot escape the retribution of the moral will. When the lights are out and we have counted sheep until we are sick of them, the "still small voice" cries out for what might have been! We travel back with hearts that are sick to the days when we dared to be righteous. We started so bravely, believing in honor and truth, sure we would keep faith with ourselves and God. We feel the blight that came, "the destruction that wasteth at noonday," [26] and we see ourselves duped by ourselves. We are unsatisfied, unfilled. We are aware that our moral aspirations are not dead—they never will be dead while God lives. We know our goodness has not perished; it endures with a tenacity we do not understand, for it roots in the goodness of God. It is "like a tree, planted by the rivers of water, that bringeth forth its fruit in its season," [27] despite the blighting drouth of our days. We must fulfill its expectations or life is dust and ashes.

We feel a coercive note in the sense of duty which bids us dare to be righteous at a price, a compulsion which suggests a will not our own. Maxwell Anderson describes it strikingly in his play, "The Eve of St. Mark," wherein Private Quizz West and his squad face death in the Philippine Islands rather than retreat to safety. In a remarkable soliloquy, reaching across the miles to his betrothed, Janet Feller, he hears her say:

[26] Psalm 91:6.
[27] Psalm 1:3.

> Who asks this of you?
> They shouldn't ask it.

Quizz answers:

> Nobody asks it, dear.
> It is something in myself I don't understand that seems
> to require it of me. It seems to be the best of me—the
> same inner self that turned to love you and no one else,
> that says give more than is asked of you . . . . . .
> We're free to go back or stay save for what's in our
> minds.[28]

Free, yet we are not free of something in ourselves we do not
understand which sends us down dangerous roads, loyal to
a duty we gladly would defy if we could and still respect ourselves. No one would have blamed Quizz and his sick and
wounded comrades if they had retreated to safety in face of
the odds against them—no one but themselves.

So the righteous who risk persecution are impelled by a
divine will that is Lord of their lives. It is something in
themselves yet reaching beyond themselves. They find no
peace save in following where the Master leads, no joy in living except in loyalty to the best they know. Theirs is "the
kingdom of heaven" because they are at one with God in
whose moral will they find their rest.

V

Righteous risk for the Master's sake leads us to the threshold
of the Kingdom of God and yields an inward fruit whose
possession is indeed blessed. Nothing else gives us the right
to self-respect. Do you recall how miserable you felt the last
time you were silent when decency called for a word from
you? You felt soiled inside and ashamed of your fear to
speak. You would give almost anything if you could go back

[28] *The Eve of St. Mark,* by Maxwell Anderson, Anderson House,
Washington, D.C., 1942, p. 190-1.

and say what you should have said. The principle works in reverse, too, as it did for a boyhood friend who arrived at school one day with a very black eye. He was a mild, friendly little fellow who got along with everybody, but he had stood up to the neighborhood bully who tried to turn a garden hose on two little girls. He came out second best in the fight, but he was proud as punch of his black eye. He took a long chance for the sake of his conviction concerning what was chivalrous, and his black eye was a symbol of his right to respect himself. Persecuted for righteousness' sake, he inherited the kingdom of self-respect. So do we all. Our willingness to be hurt for the sake of goodness is the badge of our dignity in God.

We cannot respect the coward in ourselves when He takes possession of our lives and drives us into the darkness of a dubious silence. The undying "Hero in the Soul" rebels at the base betrayal of righteousness, and conflict rages in the self. The soul's dignity rests on the soul's integrity, the self's unity on the mind's courageous honesty. The right to self-respect is the reward of righteous risk. It is a "pearl of great price," worth all that a man has. "Who choosest me must give and hazard all he hath!" Such is the kingdom's price. It is not enough to be filled with mercy and purity and peace, or even to possess an inward righteousness. Self-respect demands the courage to endure under provocation and persecution. It is the trying of faith that "worketh patience," [29] says James, and he adds, "Let this patience have a perfect work in order that ye may be perfect and entire, wanting in nothing." [30] The self is both discovered and made mature by the hurts it endures for the sake of righteousness. "We glory in the tribulations also," [31] Paul wrote. It was not a matter of pride, but a way to endurance, experience, and hope. So is it by way of harsh

[29] James 1:3.
[30] James 1:4.
[31] Romans 5:3.

opposition and hurt that we win the qualities of character that give us the right to self-respect.

Our readiness to risk suffering for the sake of righteousness is the only means by which we win the world's grudging but honest respect. Paul's change of heart on the Damascus Road had been prepared by the resolute courage of Stephen, meeting the stones of his persecutors with forgiveness in his heart. No doubt, too, as Paul laid waste the homes of Jerusalem Christians, he was troubled by their readiness to risk life itself for the sake of their faith. Haunted by the memory of men who would not quail, would not recant, who went on preaching the gospel despite threat and sword, Paul set out for Damascus with a grudging respect for those he sought to destroy. The world has no love for its Benedict Arnolds, who change their loyalties with their company. Nobody really admires the pussy-foot who agrees with everybody and never ventures an opinion until he is sure which way the wind is blowing. "The blood of the martyrs is the seed of the church" because instinctively the human spirit responds to the courage of the righteous. How did it happen that a little handful of men and women, followers of the Christ who stood out against the Roman Empire and the pagan cults, finally won the world? Preaching did not do it. There were few great preachers and few who taught with skill. It was righteous courage, daring to be fed to lions or burned on crosses, that won the respect of an alien world. You sense the meaning of such courage in the story told by George Adam Smith [32] of a young Catholic priest he met in France. The priest, on his way to the Belgian Congo, had been to visit his mother, as he said, "for the last time." "But why for the last time?" he was asked. "Because," the priest said, "the average life of a missionary on the Congo is two and one half years." "Then why go?" came the question, and the answer, "The life that I now live, I live by faith in him who loved me and gave himself for

[32] *The Significance of the Cross,* by F. W. Dillistone, Westminster Press, 1944, p. 224.

me." [33] Heroism like that commands the world's reverence. Willingness to be hurt for Christ's sake is the charter of our right to the world's respect.

There is, then, a third creative contribution of righteous risk. It is by means of righteousness, daring to be hurt if need be, that we win the right to God's promise of care and courage. When Jesus told His followers to "take my yoke upon you, for my yoke is easy," [34] and when He insisted that "my burden is light," [35] He did not mean to suggest the adequacy of the human spirit on its own. "The easy yoke" and the light burden depend on the strength we find in God. The strong man at the circus lifts weights the average mortal cannot move. His burden is easy for him, impossible for us, because the weight of a burden is proportionate to the strength we bring to it. It is so in all life, as Jesus understood so well. He knew, however, that those who faced righteous risk would inherit the strength and the courage of God. Such was the experience of St. Paul and those who faced the fury of a pagan world. "We are pressed on every side," Paul wrote, "yet not straitened; perplexed, yet not unto despair; pursued, but not forsaken; smitten down, yet not destroyed; always bearing about in the body the dying of Jesus, that the life also of Jesus may be manifest in our body." [36] That is beyond human courage; it is the grace of God sustaining righteous risk.

Such courage is the need of our time, for the ordinary garden variety of courage is not enough. After returning from a costly air raid a pilot of the Eighth Air Command wrote, "Courage is a glut on the market these days among the ground, sea and air forces." So it is, and if sheer courage to do dangerous things were all we needed to set the world aright we could rest easy. But Paul's kind of courage was more than courage; it was courage with moral flavor and spir-

[33] Galatians 2:20.
[34] Matthew 11:29.
[35] Matthew 11:30.
[36] II Corinthians 4:8.

itual roots. His suffering was not something he had to face, but something he elected to face for the sake of a Kingdom not built with hands. He anchored his soul on Christ, and let the storms break over him. If goodness were costly and right-eousness perilous in an evil world, he could take that for the sake of making things better, and the grace of God would keep him strong. He did not matter too much to himself, so if somebody had to be hurt he could follow his Master to the cross. That was a Christian's business, and God would see him through.

That throws us back, of course, to where we began, to the first Beatitude, with its invitation to self-emptying and its affirmation of our spiritual need. It is never the self-filled who risk their lives or their fortunes for righteousness. They mat-ter too much to themselves to chance being hurt. The spiritual paupers, whose charter is their own self-confidence, do not hazard their security for justice. Self-assurance flounders be-fore the assaults of the unrighteous, and self-sufficiency falters into halting compromise. It takes the self-emptied spirit to gamble life and comfort for a cause. The humility of acknowl-edged spiritual need is required to fortify the soul for heroism and righteous risk in Jesus' name. So it is that our spiritual need, our insufficient self, keep bobbing up like unwelcome relatives to remind us of the limitations of the human spirit. Only God's strength can keep us steady when men say evil against us and drive us to the wall. The "everlasting arms" are salvation then, and God's peace an anodyne for all the hurts we suffer for His sake. The brave, who are able to endure persecution and hear "all manner of evil" spoken against them, yet fail not, have traveled a long, tortuous road. They have moved from humility, wherein they faced their spiritual need, to mourning and "godly sorrow" for their sins, to meekness and stern discipline, to hunger and thirst after righteousness, to purity of heart and honest motive, to the peace-making spirit, and on, at last, to spiritual maturity and moral competence with which to bear, if need be, the martyr's crown. It is not an easy way, for "straitened is the gate and narrow the way that leadeth unto life and few there be that find it." [37] Every step along the way we are like Mary O'Hara's magnificent horse, "Thunderhead," "fighting himself," trying to make up his mind "whether to be like Flicka or like the Albino." Along the laborious way we are saying whether there shall be a "one man revolution" wherein we become "a new creation" wrought "in the image of God."

Courage to bear onward against storms of criticism and unjust abuse and fortitude to endure in the face of persecution are spiritual achievements on one side and gifts of the grace of God on the other. We endure only as we see the invisible; we see the invisible only by way of stern discipline, seeking and finding with all our hearts. The door to spiritual competence always is open on God's side, "but there are many adversaries" [38] on man's side. It is a truth that shines in the stirring story of Shadrach, Meshach, and Abednego, recorded in the Book of Daniel. Nebuchadnezzar, the king of Babylon, commanded his artisans to make a golden image and ordered the populace to worship at its shrine. With pomp and ceremony he paraded the image and the people bowed down in worship. Three men, however, defied the king and the crowd. Shadrach, Meshach, and Abednego dared to be different and to worship only the God of Abraham and Isaac and Jacob. Brought before Nebuchadnezzar and threatened with death, the three stood staunchly against surrender to the king's will. So the king ordered a fiery furnace prepared for the recalcitrant Jews, who, in the face of death, said to Nebuchadnezzar: "If so be, our God whom we serve is able to deliver us from the fiery furnace, he will deliver us out of thy hand, O King. But if not, be it known unto thee, O King, that we will not serve thy gods, nor worship the golden image which thou hast set up." [39]

[37] Matthew 7:14.
[38] I Corinthians 16:9.
[39] Daniel 3:17-18.

So, without further ceremony, Shadrach, Meshach, and Abednego were flung into the furnace, while the mob howled its delight. The flames roared and the spectators were tense. Then Nebuchadnezzar came near to the mouth of the furnace to ask in astonishment: "Did we not cast three men bound into the midst of the fire?" His lackeys answered, "True, O King." Then said Nebuchadnezzar, "Lo, I see four men loose, walking in the midst of the fire, and they have no hurt; and the form of the fourth is like unto the son of God." [40]

There always is a fourth when good men dare to be righteous. There always is One beside us when we dare to be different or persecuted for the sake of the noblest that we know, and always He is "like unto the Son of God." The fiery furnace is impotent to destroy us, and the dragons are feeble when they are met by the sword of the spirit, bent to the purposes of God. The gates to greatness beckon, and the dragons lie in wait; but beyond the gates is the grace of God, flooding in through the open doors of the human heart.

[40] Daniel 3:25.